EMOTIONAL INTELLIGENCE MASTERY 2-IN-1

THE SPIRITUAL GUIDE FOR HOW TO ANALYZE PEOPLE & YOURSELF. IMPROVE YOUR SOCIAL SKILLS, RELATIONSHIPS AND BOOST YOUR EQ 2.0 – INCLUDES EMPATH & ENNEAGRAM GUIDES

SCARLETT MULLINS

IVES FABRE

CONTENTS

Emotional Intelligence: An Introduction   vii

    MANUSCRIPT 1: The Survival Guide for Empaths   1
    Introduction to Empathy   3
1. The Difference Between Empathy and Being An Empath   7
2. Emotional Well-Being and Health   26
3. A Quick Way To Process Pain   41
4. A Few Unhealthy Habits To Avoid If You're Struggling With Your Empathic Abilities   47
5. Embracing The Empath Experience   61
6. Empaths and Relationships   68
7. Empaths and Work   84
8. The Gift Of Being An Empath   101
9. Empaths, Spirituality and Psychic Abilities   114
10. Quick Practical Tips To Start Thriving In Life As An Empath   121
11. Your Next Best Step   136
    MANUSCRIPT 2: The Enneagram   143
    Introduction To Enneagram   145
12. Origins   148
    Section I Understanding The Basics And Background Of The System   157
13. The Theory of Enneagram   158
14. Understanding The Modern Day Enneagram of Personality Tool   162
15. Introduction To Enneagram Types   167
16. Structure Of The Diagram   170

	SECTION II The Enneagram Personality Types In Detail	184
17.	The Enneagram Of Personality Types	185
	Section III: Instincts, Subtypes and variants within the Enneagram of Personality Tool	229
18.	Diving Deeper into who you really are	230
	Section IV: Using The Enneagram To Enrich Your Life	267
19.	Integrating an ancient tool into a modern living	268
20.	Accelerating your personal growth and self-expression	271
21.	Enneagram Test	279
22.	Cultivating Healthy Loving Relationships	284
23.	Mapping out your path of most joy and fulfillment	296

© **Copyright 2019 - All rights reserved.**

The content contained within this book may not be reproduced, duplicated or transmitted without direct written permission from the author or the publisher.

Under no circumstances will any blame or legal responsibility be held against the publisher, or author, for any damages, reparation, or monetary loss due to the information contained within this book. Either directly or indirectly.

Legal Notice:

This book is copyright protected. This book is only for personal use. You can't amend, distribute, sell, use, quote or paraphrase any part, or the content within this book, without the consent of the author or publisher.

Disclaimer Notice:

Please note the information contained within this document is for educational and entertainment purposes only. All effort has been executed to present accurate, up to date, and reliable, complete information. No warranties of any kind are declared or implied. Readers acknowledge that the author isn't engaging in the rendering of legal, financial, medical or professional advice. The content within this book has been derived from various sources. Please consult a licensed professional before attempting any techniques outlined in this book.

By reading this document, the reader agrees that under no circumstances are is the author responsible for any losses, direct or indirect, which are incurred as a result of the use of information contained within this document, including, but not limited to, —errors, omissions, or inaccuracies.

EMOTIONAL INTELLIGENCE: AN INTRODUCTION

In today's world of fast-paced, "get the job done at any cost" attitudes, it can sometimes feel like you're not making the progress in your personal and professional life that you really want, despite putting in so much work.

Often, this is down to our relationships with others, and ourselves, so learning more about how relationships manifest and function at the deepest level is something that will massively benefit anyone who is looking to improve their social and professional relationships.

Emotional Intelligence could be the answer.

IQ (Intelligence Quotient) and EQ (Emotional Quotient) aim to measure the two primary forms of human intelligence and, in combination with an assessment of a person's personality, modern science aims to understand the psyche of an individual more fully.

With studies showing that people with higher levels of Emotional Intelligence enjoy a more satisfying and successful career and personal relationships, it's more and more important to understand yourself and others at this fundamental level better to achieve your life goals.

Why we wrote this book:

Given all the compelling evidence that a person's Emotional Intelligence is directly linked to their personal and professional success and happiness, we thought a great way to do this would be to bring together two of the best fields for understanding yourself, for understanding others, and ultimately, for understanding how people interact with each other at a fundamental and emotional level.

Based on various sources, Emotional intelligence (also known as Emotional Quotient, or EQ) is defined as:

"the ability to control one's own emotions and the other's emotions, distinguish between emotions and label them

appropriately, and the use of emotional information to stimulate thought and behavior."

Given this, working to understand yourself and the emotions of others, as well as gaining an appreciation of the different personality types, and how they interact with each other, will give you a massive advantage when working to improve your relationships, your career, and your happiness.

It's to this end that we've put together (in our opinion) the two most critical distinct subjects that can help you achieve these goals:

- ***The Survival Guide For Empaths*** - So you can learn to control your own emotions and feel strong, capeable and confident in any situation.
- ***The Enneagram*** - To help you understand the different personality types at their deepest level, and how they each interact with each other so you'll always know the "right" way to handle any interaction.

With these two fantastic resources, you'll learn exactly how to take control of your own emotions, how to read and understand other's emotions and how different personality types interact with each other. Armed with this knowledge, you'll be fully prepared to build a happier, wealthier and more rewarding life.

So what are you waiting for? Let's get started!

MANUSCRIPT 1: THE SURVIVAL
GUIDE FOR EMPATHS

The Survival Guide for Empaths:
The Beginners Survival Guide Book for Healing a
Highly Sensitive Person

INTRODUCTION TO EMPATHY

In a world where emotions have often been associated with weakness, it can be pretty tough coping in society if you're an empath. It's even worse when (like I used to be) you don't even know you're an empath, because often what happens is you invariably find yourself trapped in emotions, relationships, or environments that suck the life out of you.

Dealing with your emotions (and those of others) in a world that doesn't appreciate or value your sensitivities can be overwhelming and very detrimental to your wellbeing. There's a real sense of suffocation and powerlessness that accompanies this challenge which must be addressed and dealt with as early on in life as possible, otherwise, happiness becomes a daunting task.

This book and all the information contained is made for the sole purpose of helping you, the reader, finally come to a new understanding of what it really means to be an Empath.

Sure you've seen a lot of people talk about it. Both science and spirituality seem to have strong concepts around what it means to be an empath. But you know what? At the end of the day, only an empath can fully understand what it feels like to go through daily human living as such. And as far as I can see, there isn't much knowledge given in the way of navigating successfully this path of being an empath. At best we find material that seems to increase confusion or promote a lifestyle that feels isolating and unsatisfying.

So if like me you want to enjoy life to the fullest while still honoring the subtle differences that enable you to perceive human living through a different lens, then may this book aid you in meeting that end.

Here's what this book is not:

Before we get started here's some clarity regarding what you can expect from reading this book and what it won't be about. This isn't about some gendered nonsense isolating one from the other as I find that to be utterly unnecessary since research in HSP (highly sensitive people) shows that there is no difference between men and women.

It will neither excuse nor encourage behavior that is inexcusable and it's not about elevating empaths over "normal" people. I have no interest in seeing you live an isolated life and I certainly don't want to aid you in "avoiding" anything that would actually promote a healthier, happier human experience. I feel you already know all too well what to avoid. You certainly don't need my help with that!

But what you probably need is greater clarity on how you can enrich your life and stretch beyond the current comfort zone that abstracts the freedom you can feel in burning up your heart.

This is my intention in writing this book. If you resonate with the idea of overcoming the limitations that society often places on those of us who are highly sensitive and gifted with empathic abilities, then it's time for us to begin this journey.

Pace yourself. Trust in this process and know that

you will emerge more fearless, and empowered if you open-mindedly absorb the ideas contained in each chapter.

Shall we begin?

1

THE DIFFERENCE BETWEEN EMPATHY AND BEING AN EMPATH

"When you start to develop your powers of empathy and imagination, the whole world opens up to you"

- Susan Sarandon.

Empathy is a trait that can be learned by anyone. And to some extent we all practice empathy in varying degrees as we interact with each other. But showing empathy and being an empath are actually not identical.

Here's how to process the difference between the two.

Imagine you are sitting down at Starbucks with two

of your friends that you very much adore. Both strong in character and while different in personalities you know they both have big hearts.

Suddenly a couple sitting next to you cause a scene. The guy bangs the table in anger spilling a perfectly wonderful Frappuccino all over and yells a few words before stomping out. The woman left behind feels utterly crushed and embarrassed. Tears stream down her red cheeks and she hangs her head as low as possible as she quickly tries to clean up the mess created. For a moment, all eyes are on her and you could literally feel everything that she felt.

One of your friends turns to you and asks, "Should we go over there and see if we can help?" As you look over to your friend you notice her cheeks are flushed and her eyes are just as teary as yours. It's almost as if you're both experiencing what the couple experienced. Before you can even respond, your other friend jumps in and says, *"Naaa, she'll be fine. Look she's already stopped crying. Let it go."*

What just happened in that scenario?

One of your friends did show some empathy and recognized the discomfort of the woman but that's as far as it went. She was glad to just get on with her day as if nothing happened. The other friend, however, seemed to have had a completely different experience. Her entire body chemistry changed. And you felt it too, didn't you?

This is the subtle difference between showing empathy and being an empath.

Empathy is the ability to understand and share the feelings of another. With a little conscious effort, every human being has the ability to demonstrate empathy when the situation calls for it.

When one is an empath, however, it's an entirely different experience. It's more like having an elevated gift and an ability to step into another person's shoes. An empath has the power to step outside his or her own experience and understand what another person is saying, thinking, and feeling. It's more than just being a highly sensitive person and it goes beyond sensing emotions.

According to science, empaths are highly sensitive and can process emotions faster and more intimately. The common acronym for this is HSP meaning a Highly Sensitive Person. A highly sensitive person isn't to be confused with an attention seeker or overly sensitive people who enjoy unpleasant tantrum infused behaviors. It means you are high in sensory processing sensitivity. A true HSP is usually very aware of the feelings of others and very reluctant to cause a scene.

So, as you may have guessed from the example I shared of your two friends, one of them does demonstrate empathy, which is great. But the other friend is more likely to be considered an empath.

A true empath goes beyond being a HSP; he or she also has empathic abilities which, when mastered, result in a very powerful being capable of various things such as healing others. But we'll get into that a little later in the book.

The natural question that follows is: how does one know whether they possess empathic abilities or not?

I mean, do you actually know if you're an empath? How about we finally shed some light on that.

A Self-diagnosis answering one question: Am I An Empath?

"I think we all have empathy. We may not have enough courage to display it."

-Maya Angelou

I grew up like most kids with parents who wanted me to fit in and be like all the other kids. Except I just wasn't like the other kids. Being on my own made me feel better. I couldn't stand being in large crowds. Growing up I remember watching something on television that was a particularly bad story and it totally freaked me out. I don't recall exactly what the bad story was about, but I do remember how shocked my mother was when 3 hours later she found me still locked up in my room sobbing hysterically.

These "incidents" kept showing up into my adult years, sometimes causing me to spend days in complete isolation feeling very misunderstood by everyone including my partner. For a while I had a roommate and I could feel their resentment and anger each time they walked through the door. It was almost like I as breathing in the energy of whoever was near me at any given point in time.

It was tough. People just called me moody, too sensitive and unpredictable. Growing up I was told I needed to grow thicker skin and stop taking everything so personally. But that's because no one in my environment took the time to understand what was really happening inside me.

It's not easy going through daily life feeling like no one gets you. You know?

Truth be told, as I get older and mature it is becoming evident that there are various levels of being empathic. It's almost like a spectrum with varying degrees from the highest (true empaths with healing abilities) to those who are suffering from a serious deficiency (narcissists). There are people who are highly sensitive and keenly aware of all the different energies around them and there are those who've taken it to a whole new level where it's almost as though the surrounding energies of others overpower them. They feel in their bodies the same feeling whether good or bad that another is experiencing.

These are the people who will often report this experience of other people's feelings becoming intrusive and uncontrollable. Regardless of how chronic your empathic levels are, it is prudent to do a self-assessment to get more in touch with who you really are.

So here are reflective questions to help you in this quest to understand why you feel and experience life as you do. Keep in mind this list of questions is just an overview to help you get that initial clarity.

If you would like to dive deeper into yourself then I recommend having a conversation with a coach or an empathy expert. As a general rule of thumb, if you answer yes to at least 6 of these 12 questions, you are definitely an empath with amazing gifts that need to be utilized positively in the world.

1. Am I usually drawn to animals and can sense their emotions?

2. Do I often feel overwhelmed in large crowds or in the presence of others?

3. Am I powerfully drawn to people experiencing emotional pain?

4. Do I need to seclude myself from others on a regular basis for some downtime?

5. Am I often dreaming vividly of future events and do my dreams often come to pass?

6. Can I usually tell when someone is not being honest or authentic?

7. Do I possess any healing powers?

8. Does finding time for self-care often feel like a struggle for me?

9. Do I consider myself a free spirit with distaste for control, rules, and routine?

10. Am I constantly struggling with my body weight?

11. Do I have a strong creative streak and a vivid imagination?

12. Is strong violence, cruelty of any kind or tragedy utterly unbearable to me?

Congratulations!

Now you know more about who you really are. If you answered yes to most if not all of the 12 questions, you not only have empathic abilities but you also have the opportunity to make a special difference in our present world.

Yes, it is true. Empaths are having a particularly difficult time in our fast-paced modern world. There's a lot of negativity being broadcasted and unfortunately, they come right at you. But be of good cheer, for all hope is not lost. There is much work ahead of us if we want to turn things around and stop falling victim to the negative emotions being emanated.

This gift you have just discovered and validated is a

blessing. But in order for you to harness and enjoy it as such, you will need more awareness on how to groom yourself so you can walk around this earth as a positive force for good, healing those that require and request it, breathing into the atmosphere the nourishing energies that bring about prosperity, and playing your part as a loving, gifted being.

That is the new chapter of your life that awaits you, which is why I encourage to keep turning the pages of this book and discover how to elevate yourself to the point of thriving as an empath.

How does empathy show up and what are the effects?

Most of the time the things you might experience as you go through daily living may not make much sense to you and others around you especially if you don't know you're an empath.

Oftentimes empaths feel like the weight of the world is on their shoulder. There's a tone of heaviness, sadness, anxiety, depression and a general feeling of discomfort that's always looming in the background of everything they do.

I remember when I first landed my dream job working with a fast growing entertainment company that had establishments in America, Europe, and Africa. My friendships and family relationships were great and I loved my job. It was the first time I was part of something so big and could afford living in a big beautiful apartment in Jersey. To an outside observer, I had a perfect life.

But there was a discomfort I just couldn't shake and there was this burdensome feeling constantly accompanying me. Most of my evenings were spent trying to deal with this enormous fatigue that even sleep wasn't curing. What was wrong?

Still unaware of my abilities, I didn't take cognizance of the various ways they were showing up in my daily life. So I kept bumping into conditions and circumstances that were creating very negative subtle sensations that impacted me.

Now your case might be different.

You could be experiencing discomfort more related to your health or relationships. Many people with empathic abilities report various health struggles and diseases such as agoraphobia, chronic fatigue, allergies, and fibromyalgia.

On an emotional level, the commonality that we see tends to be experiences of anxiety, depression and even panic attacks. It could also be that you notice every time someone around you gets ill, you quickly pick up the same symptoms. Even simple things like regularly catching colds from others could be an effect of being a blind empath. You might also be getting periodic blurred vision that you just can't explain. Almost like there's a subtle invisible layer preventing your eyes from seeing clearly.

And because we are usually so immersed in the feelings and stresses that others are experiencing, our personal self-care is often neglected because we forget to work on our true inner needs since there's always layers from other people covering our real inner needs.

Other areas where you may need to observe to see what's showing up are:

your relationships, love and sexual experiences. If you find yourself recreating relationships that are toxic, unhealthy and unproductive, this could be due to your empathic abilities that haven't yet been harnessed and controlled. We'll dive more into this in an upcoming chapter.

But here's something you need to remember. When you walk around unconsciously being controlled by your special abilities you'll often get sucked into partners and experiences that end up hurting you.

The tendency to overindulge or become addicted may also be an issue to watch out for. Empaths usually turn to addictions such as food, sex, drugs, alcohol, or even shopping in order to block out their sensitivities. Many struggle with weight issues because that extra padding is used as a defense mechanism to protect against negative energy.

Judith Orloff M.D and author of emotional freedom offers an energetic theory of obesity: "When empaths are thin, they have less padding and are more vulnerable to absorbing stress. Early-twentieth-century faith healers were renowned for being grossly obese to avoid taking on their patients' symptoms, a common trap I've seen modern healing practitioners also unconsciously fall into; food is a grounding device." ("Judith Orloff M.D., The Energy of Food: A Missing Piece In Weight Loss, 'n.d.'")

She also adds that many of her patients gain weight to protect against stress at home and at work. Your perceptual abilities, vivid dreams, ability to sense people's energy and a powerful intuition are not to be ignored. These show up in your daily life because your high sensitivities can interpret and perceive things at a heightened level. The more you learn to harness your powers, the more empowered you'll become to use them in a positive grounded way.

The effects you will experience will very much vary depending on how developed and nurtured your empathic abilities are. And what you'll notice is that the more you learn to appreciate and effectively utilize your gifts, the more joyous and liberated you'll feel.

Of course, there is a very positive and nourishing effect of being an empath. And they too will show up in your daily life. Learn to spot these and pour more attention on the positive special effects that you become aware of.

This can be an increased sense of creativity in the things you feel passionate about. It can also be your ability to be a great leader and team player. Yes, even if you're an introvert, you can still be a great leader because you're more inclined to notice the little details that others miss. Your ability to sense what others feel also makes you a major asset at work because you'll deal with people fairly and with true understanding.

The special resonance you oftentimes feel with

nature, gardens, water or the bond you may feel with animal companions and people in need makes you a marvelous individual. It opens you up to the richness of nature and enables you to always see the bigger picture in life.

As you can see, the list is endless and the more you intentionally go into your day seeking out these positive effects, the longer your list becomes. So I definitely encourage you to start making that list because contrary to what you were told growing up, empathic abilities are not something to be ashamed of.

This is whom you were born to be and it's about time you unapologetically embrace the real you.

The false ideas you need to shed about being an empath

There are so many myths and false concepts that have circulated over years around being an empath and I feel many of these ideas actually make it hard for us to live empowered lives. Let's start debunking a few of these and see if any of them hit a nerve for you.

False Idea #1: Being an empath is a totally spiritual thing

This is definitely a basic misconception that segregates empaths. While the lines do sometimes cross over between science and spirituality you absolutely don't need to be spiritual, religious or a spiritual healer to be an empath.

In the book *'The Empath's Survival Guide'* Judith Orloff starts off saying that empaths have a hyperactive mirror neuron system so that we are able to sense what other people are going through, and that narcissists have empathy deficient disorder. That's a scientific fact, not spiritual speculation.

My Truth:

Scientific research has proven the existence of empaths. To be fair, this is a very new study in the world of science and we barely understand the neurology behind empathy in general. But new research is surfacing supporting the existence of empaths.

Dr. Michel Banissy, a Professor of Psychology at Goldsmiths, and his post-doctoral researcher, Dr. Natalie Bowling have spent years looking into empathy and mirror-touch synaesthesia. Though we still have a long way to go, findings are showing between one and two percent of the population does report experiencing conditions associated with being empathic.

And the fact still holds true. My brain will demonstrate empathic abilities whether I'm spiritually inclined or not. Therefore understanding empaths isn't supposed to be some esoteric wishy-washy impractical thing.

False Idea #2: Empathic abilities are a disorder or mental illness

While it is true that we oftentimes get hit with overwhelming situations and scenarios that leave us feeling physically sick, it is certainly not true that empaths suffer from mental disorders or anything of that kind.

My Truth:

The emotions and physical sensations you have are nothing to be ashamed of. There is nothing wrong with you! You are not sick or crazy.

Let me say that again...

Don't be put to shame or feel less than because you possess abilities to perceive far greater things than the general public. The human population has become so desensitized it's easier to label and categorize those groups of people that don't fit into the model view of the status quo such as empath who possess powers of higher perception.

False Idea #3: Being an empath means you're weak and playing the victim

Emotions are for wimps and overly sensitive people. Bet you've heard that all your life. This false belief has been pervading human consciousness for centuries. Showing your emotions is often seen as a sign of weakness. A lot of people assume that empaths are weak powerless and co-dependent on others. Many believe empaths live in a state of victimhood always fearful of the world around them.

Revealing to people your truth and what you can sense in them is so scary for people that are disconnected from their own emotions, they often call you a freak. Perhaps this is why most empaths become recluse.

My Truth:

All these misconceptions are generalized biases and nothing close to the truth. The fact that we are able to quickly process emotions and sensations that the majority of the population does not understand doesn't mean we are weaker. If anything we pay more attention to the feelings of others and pay a lot of attention to how we treat others. There's no need for you to ever justify or get offended when someone rejects who you are. Just remember for most people, your way of being is incomprehensible and illogical to their mind.

And when it comes to taking responsibility, bouncing back from challenges and working hard to make a difference, empaths perform just as well as any other human being. An empath can be just as strong, responsible and successful in the world as anyone else, so don't let other people's limitations or fears cause you to settle for anything less than what your heart desires.

False Idea #4: Empaths are all introverts.

It appears to be that the majority of empaths are introverts but this is certainly not true across the board.

My Truth:

Individuals bearing all kinds of characteristics will possess empathic abilities. Don't feel like you have to "fit" into a particular category of anything in order to exercise your empathic gifts. You can be an extrovert, introvert, ambivert or none of the above and still be an empath.

The idea of introversion as a prerequisite for being an empath is simply not true.

Now that you've shed some of the false notions that may have played a role in constricting you, take a moment to see if any other myths come up. I encourage you to write them down on a piece of paper and right next to them write your truth. Convert all the active false beliefs in your mind about what it means to be an empath into constructive ideas that will nourish a healthy mindset as you move on to the next chapter.

EMOTIONAL WELL-BEING AND HEALTH

"Health is a relationship between you and your body."

- Unknown

Since we all know that being an empath is all about energy and our sensitivities, doesn't it make complete sense to be more proactive when it comes to managing the energies relating to our health and well-being?

Unfortunately, the information that is abundantly shared online is more focused on "hiding" and "protecting" myself from the world.

To me, there's a fundamental flaw in this mindset,

because by only focusing on hiding myself or creating defensive strategies that keep the negative stuff out I am essentially giving my power of attention and intention to the very thing I do not want.

Think about it for a minute. "*Let me build a strong defense and shield for myself*" cannot be the only solution. It's good for immediate and temporary relief when faced with unexpected danger but it cannot be a long-term solution. It won't help me thrive or live a freedom based lifestyle because the activated vibration in this thought pattern is - I pick up negativity all the time.

Here's the thing.

When you are an empath it's like being a sponge absorbing everything in your environment. But you don't have to be a walking human sponge or fall victim to this gift. You do have the power to be a highly sensitive person, but you can be capable of interpreting and sensing energy at a heightened level and still be the master controlling what enters your domain of authority and what is kept out.

Not only that, but you also have the power to enhance your abilities so that you emanate and "pick up vibrations" that are predominantly good for you. Did you know that?

Can you imagine how much better your world could become if you found this balance?

Your power becomes endless.

Deepak Chopra says understanding your unique mind-body type, or dosha, and learning how to make the right choices to reestablish balance is crucial if you want to enjoy great health. In an article response to one of Oprah.com's followers where the question posed was by a 43 year old woman who was experiencing anxiety and overwhelm as she felt her world crumbling over, Chopra's response was very simple and informative.

"In the system of traditional Indian medicine known as Ayurveda, one of the basic elements in a persons makeup is known as Vayu, or wind. It gives rise to a quality known as Vata, the aspect of the mind and body associated with spontaneity, change, resilience and vitality. When Vata is out of balance, restlessness, worry, confusion, indecision, anxiety and a general inability to settle down or see straight arise. ("Ask Deepak: How to find balance when you're feeling overwhelmed, April 2010")

As you may have guessed, most of us struggle with many if not all of these symptoms and it's not meant to be a normal way of life for us. We need to get to the root of the problem and bring back that balance.

The key to doing that is to begin recognizing that you might have patterns of behavior that do not align with your true nature. The more you get into harmony with your own individual power, find balance and work on raising your own energy, the easier it becomes to match yourself up with well-being and a healthy lifestyle. It starts with acquiring a new set of beliefs and a new perspective.

If you believe your powers make you weak and that you are at the mercy of everything and everyone in the world that will be your dominant energy. And it's going to be tough creating any other reality.

What do you believe about your emotions and empathic abilities?

Understanding and controlling emotions

Modern society continues to do us a great disservice when it comes to understanding and controlling our emotions even though science shows a direct correlation between great health and balanced emotions.

Because we've also inherited some debilitating patterns of thought, whenever there's conflict within, rather than taking the time to process the emotions, we often block them off and attempt to suck it up.

Thwarting emotions is very unhealthy both physically and mentally especially for empaths who are always highly sensitive. So let's get back to basics with this topic.

What are feelings and emotions and why do they matter?

Contrary to what most people think, feelings and emotions are not one and the same.

An emotion is a chemical that gets released when we interpret a specific stimulus. A feeling is the integration of that released emotion and we begin to become cognizant of the effects or consequence of the released emotion in our bodies and brain. Then a feedback loop gets created whereby that feeling causes more release of emotions and our intensity of feeling increases in the process.

It's important for us to have emotions because this is what helps us interpret the raw data about the world around us and our feelings help us create meaning out of the data that we perceive. It goes without saying that for us as empaths, gaining mastery over the interpretation of the emotions we receive is vital. Equally as important is the fact that we need to gain emotional intelligence and develop filtering abilities so that as we process that highly sensitive psychological experience that is constantly taking place while we are exposed to other people, animals and the environment we need to hone in the ability to quickly "sort out" and identify the energies that we want to allow into our energetic space and those that we want to release as quickly as possible to avoid getting hurt.

Most empaths want to know if they can choose to only feel good energies.

Well, actually you can. But the way you get to the level where you can discern and choose to predominantly interact and match up with only good energies depends on your emotional resilience.

Having the power of choice means you must be exposed to options from which you can pick and choose what you desire. So if you're looking to experience the best of the empathic experience, you need to stop running away from the negative (by running away you're giving it power over you) and instead grow into your power so that nothing you don't choose can take over your space. That requires diligence and practice. You need a lot of self-awareness, self-love and self-understanding.

Your emotions are your guiding system. They help you navigate this human experience. How you feel at any given time is the conscious awareness of the frequency you are broadcasting to the universe whether that emotion originated with you or not.

When your mind impedes the flow of emotions because they are either too overwhelming or conflicting, that affects your body and produces a psychological distress and symptoms, which if left unchecked can turn into chronic physical and mental illness.

Emotional stress and blocked energies have been linked to mental illness and physical problems like digestive issues, back problems, heart disease, migraines, autoimmune disorders, insomnia and so much more. The Journal of Psychiatry published a study they conducted in which they found that empaths are more susceptible to depression, and anxiety in general. The study concluded that socially anxious individuals may demonstrate a unique social cognitive abilities profile with elevated cognitive empathy tendencies and a high accuracy in affective mental state attributions. It is this hyper-sensitivity to emotions that may also cause empaths to become ill more often than others when not properly managed.

The more self-aware you become of your own emotions and better handle them the easier it becomes to control and handle all the other emotions you pick up when interacting with the world. It's time to stop glossing over how you really feel about yourself.

Do you feel safe in this world?

Do you feel misunderstood?

Do you feel alone and at the mercy of energies that are more powerful than you?

You are more powerful than you think and you have the ability to control so much more than you realize.

Can you stop empathic abilities if you're tired of feeling emotionally drained and don't want that power anymore?

The short answer is, no. There's no stopping your gift. In this life, you don't get a choice over creation. As long as you are breathing and walking in that human body you will continue to co-create with life. The details and quality of that creation are entirely up to you but you can't be able to stop or pause it.

All the gifts that you came to earth with are yours as long as you journey this human experience. You get to choose how little or how much to use them. And they can become a burden or a blessing, even that is entirely up to you. Wanting to put an end to your ability to sense other people and the environment is a fight you cannot win because, in the web of life, we are all connected. The only difference is some of us are more acutely aware of that connection than others.

What you would rather focus on is how to handle your emotions master your mind and better filter out the energies that you interact with as you go through your day. These are all things you can easily learn which will, in turn, help you better relate to the different sensations and energies around you in a constructive way.

Learning to stop absorbing other people's symptoms

Soon after being introduced to the man that I thought would be my true soul mate, it became clear to me that something wasn't right. Sure the intimacy felt incredible and I was totally smitten but I started noticing a pattern.

After spending a weekend with him I would find myself on Sunday night curled up on my bed with the same flu he'd just caught. Oftentimes date night would be fun, but gosh it would drain the life out of me. I would justify the chronic fatigue and heaviness in various ways but not once did I suspect I was simply absorbing his overly cynical and negative outlook on life and people. I felt like I was giving, giving and giving some more but he wasn't willing to give anything back.

Our dinner conversations spanned a variety of topics from politics to the current state of social media much of which I was merely a silent listener trying to understand this man with whom I was deeply in love.

Unfortunately, as the weeks turned to months, my health, emotional stability, and overall well-being started taking a serious downturn.

Now, I'm not pointing fingers or blaming him for anything. I merely want to show you how sometimes the people closest to us can become catalysts to a lot of agonizing pain even without knowing it.

He wasn't necessarily a bad guy and I'm sure for any other woman it wouldn't be an issue. But when you're an open sponge with a porous body that absorbs everything in your environment, the people you spend the most time with can become a massive liability. This doesn't mean you become a lone wolf. Far from it.

As I have learned over the years, it's more about learning to ground yourself and setting healthy boundaries that enable you to process emotions better and filter out the pain, stress, and conflicts that go on around you.

But first, you need to have the realization that this is actually happening in your life. You can't live in denial just because you care about someone.

Here's the most important thing to always remember:

When you realize there's a pattern in your life where certain people, situations or triggers result in physical discomfort that cannot be medically diagnosed, know that you're not imagining things or going crazy. You are simply a highly sensitive person with a gift that must be developed, nurtured and successfully managed.

The whole purpose of learning to embrace your empathic abilities and becoming a true empath is so that you can stop being at the mercy of other people's pain, stresses, and conflicts.

Highly sensitive people absorb anything and everything and oftentimes they have no control over it. A true empath has mastered his or her abilities and doesn't automatically get overwhelmed by the emotions of another. This is how I've personally redefined for myself what it means to be an empath. How are you going to redefine it for yourself?

If you are truly ready to gain mastery over your special abilities then it's time to equip yourself with simple living strategies that will empower and help you center yourself so you can finally stop absorbing other people's dysfunctions.

1. Use the power of your breath.

First, you need to realize the power contained in your breathing. Whenever you suspect you're picking up someone else's symptoms, bring all your focused attention to your breath for a few minutes. Surrender to this simple act of breathing deeply in and out. Use it to ground yourself and connect to your power.

2. Name it to tame it.

Next, ask yourself - what is this emotional or physical distress I am feeling? Whenever we put a label on something we decrease the momentum of the impact, which gives us ample time to constructively handle the issue.

3. Evaluate it "in the moment".

Once you've brought it to the forefront of your mind, evaluate this emotion. Don't let this slide and take over your mind and body. Deal with it immediately before it grows into a monster.

Is the distress really yours or have you picked it up from something or someone? Sometimes the answer is both. If for example you're feeling deep fear and it's yours, gently confront what's causing it. And you can do this either on your own or by getting professional help. If however, you realize it isn't yours, pinpoint the obvious generator and work on releasing it.

4. Take a step back.

This can be physically moving away so you can get

into a mindful space to handle the situation or it can be a mental movement. Either way, you want to be able to create some movement that allows you to start reaching for that sense of relief that's absolutely essential in releasing unwanted energies.

5. Become more aware of your mind-body connection.

Keep breathing deeply. Seek to find where in your body you feel most vulnerable. Chances are if you can find that spot where the alarm is going off you can quickly turn things around and step back into your power. The more you practice this exercise the better you'll know how your body works.

For example, in my case, my solar plexus is where I go first because I know my tummy is always the first place my alarm hits. By the time I start feeling it on my left shoulder I know it's reached stage two which means the issue is more serious and I need to do something fast.

The physical sensations may not be identical but the same rule will be true for you. Our bodies are such wonderful communicators. We just need to get better at understanding the signals they send.

So let's suppose for you it's a migraine headache or a

sore throat, the moment you become aware of these symptoms, sit in silence, relax your entire mind and body. Practice your deep breathing. Place the palm of your hand on the area and practice soothing yourself, giving yourself self-healing. Keep doing it and speaking with yourself until the discomfort dissipates. In the last chapter of this book you'll find lots of other useful practices to test out.

If you've been battling with depression, panic attacks or chronic pain for a long time, this simple method when done daily with intention will strengthen and comfort you. It's a great way to reconnect your mind and body and imbue yourself with that feeling of safety that we all need. No one can heal you better than you can heal yourself. Learn to trust that.

3

A QUICK WAY TO PROCESS PAIN

*P*ain is a huge topic for empaths especially because most of the reports, stories and information currently available present a very dull and gloomy world for an empath.

Dealing with pain head-on is no easy task but it is crucial for us to learn how to become warriors when it comes to pain and suffering because of our health, longevity, and well-being depend on it.

I am starting to think one of the main reasons empaths are often associated with constant depression, anxiety, and fatigue attacks is because they usually don't know how to deal with emotions of anger, pain, and suffering. Rather than handle them in healthy ways, they tend to absorb and suppress.

But did you know your emotions could be processed and metabolized the same way you process food? That's what I want to teach you right now.

Derived from the Greek word "em" (in) and "pathos" (feeling), the term empathic means you and I can "feel into" others' feelings. It means we are highly tuned in, sensitive and capable of absorbing the energy being transmitted by the other. It makes us vulnerable to what science has termed as 'emotional contagion', which simply means you will absorb the emotions of whomever you interact with. The major issue with that is we live in a world inundated with false ideas, negativity and a lot of emotional torture. So pain and silent suffering is a vibration a lot of people are carrying around and when exposed to it, whether we filter it out quickly or not, it still impacts us.

A large part of the anxiety, depression and chronic pain that is so common among empaths actually belongs to the collective consciousness; the current stress, and suffering that humanity is undergoing. But most people have literally been conditioned into emotional illiteracy and they've numbed themselves out from "feeling" their own emotional broadcasts. But that doesn't mean they don't broadcast that energy anyways and you know what sucks? You and your heightened sensitivities will pick it up immediately upon encountering such a person. Then you'll be stuck with the burden of having to deal with that pain.

Do you know how to release pain and suffering from your energetic field in a healthy way?

I learned this lesson the hard way. There was a time in my life when I was just a human sponge walking around absorbing sensations I didn't care for. It all felt completely out of my control. I was always tired and in pain. Something was always aching in my body and pain relievers became my very good friends. It wasn't until I joined a Yoga class where my instructor who took a very holistic approach to life enlightened me on what was happening. My muscle tension, constant body aches and continued migraine were all effects of accumulated pain that I was holding on to.

Whether it was my own or absorbed from another, that pain was causing major issues in my functionality, but I didn't know it was possible to release it in healthy ways. Since I know empaths constantly have to deal with a lot of challenging energies, let me share the simple process I have been using ever since to release and clear off the pain and toxicity.

1. Take responsibility for the emotions you're experiencing. Whether or not the energy originated from you or someone else, it's in your energetic field now impacting your body, so take full responsibility for it.

2. Witness the emotions in your body. Feel your body with your eyes closed. Notice where it is and how it feels. Do your best to define it in present first tense and refrain from using words that victimize you. *For example, rather than say, I feel hurt (a victim mentality that disempowers you) choose to say, I am feeling hurting or I am angry etc.*

3. Now describe the thing or situation surrounding this feeling in the first person and how you're experiencing it.

4. Describe it in the second person as if you were an observer of that particular scenario.

5. Describe the same situation and feelings again but this time in the third person as if you were a reporter writing for a magazine and notice how detached you now feel about the entire thing.

You may choose to carry out this exercise verbally or by writing it down on paper. If you write it down, be sure to make it ceremonial in the end by shredding it up into pieces or burning the paper and openly declare, "I release you and let you go. I now welcome universal divine love and fresh energy to fill my entire being. Do some mindful breathing and once you "feel the shift" that's it! It is done. Now put on a song and dance in celebration or treat yourself to a cupcake (that would be me).

The key here is to notice how you feel at every stage of this process.

Pain and toxic emotions are not states we need to be afraid of or get tormented by when we come across them. We just need to know they are harmful to our health and well-being and learn to quickly spot and release them.

Unfortunately, there's a lot of pain and suffering floating around our planet. This is why it's so important to notice how you feel in your interaction with others. Learn to clean up your energy often and create rituals around your daily life that help you stay grounded as you interact with the world.

Influencing others emotionally:

The more you learn to become an empathic warrior always grounded in your true power the easier it becomes for you to start positively influencing others emotionally.

Where there is pain and suffering, you can pour in joy and hope. Where there is anger you can pour in affection and peace. Where there is any fear you can cast it out with the energy of love that radiates from within you. If we are to heal our planet it can only be as a result of learning to overcome our own darkness and becoming so bright that our light starts to shine on others as well.

Your ability to sense and connect with the energy of another human being or animal doesn't just make you vulnerable, it also makes them vulnerable to whatever you're broadcasting. And if you're vibrational offering is higher and stronger in frequency, you can perform amazing miracles for people without them ever realizing what you've done. Think of the good you can do in the world once you master this.

A FEW UNHEALTHY HABITS TO AVOID IF YOU'RE STRUGGLING WITH YOUR EMPATHIC ABILITIES

"Our bodies are our gardens – our wills are our gardeners."

- William Shakespeare

The struggle is real; no one can deny that. It is a journey and a challenging one at that. Figuring out a healthy way to express yourself in the world, while simultaneously handling your emotions as well as the energies of those around you is no easy task and no one should ever make light of the path you are walking. It takes more than mere willpower to successfully do it.

I know how easy overwhelm and anxiety can creep

up in my day and I've seen my friends really struggle to get a grip sometimes. Which is why I always encourage empaths to stop being so hard on themselves when they do get stuck in a coping mechanism that isn't actually helpful.

Unfortunately most of the habits we tend to form only make things worse in the long run and as a result, we end up intensifying the already challenging journey of being an empath in this world. I believe no one deserves to go through daily life feeling anxious, defeated and at the mercy of coping mechanisms. So let me shed some light on some unhealthy things that I have seen fellow empaths struggling with in the hopes that you will avoid these habits or eliminate them as soon as you spot them.

The aim here is to make you a mighty, empowered empath and valuable member in your community not a self-loathing "coping addict".

Marijuana and empaths

I know it's a common practice. Smoking weed does help numb out and dim down all the noise we constantly pick up. Many empaths just feel way better with a daily dose no matter how small. But here's the thing. If you're smoking as a means to escape, the consequences of that decision can never be good.

It's a great temporary relief, but you know what? So is scrolling through your Facebook feed for an entire afternoon or binge-watching Netflix. Doesn't mean you should be doing it. As soon as you step back into reality the same pain, angst, frustration will still be there. That temporary fix does not resolve anything. At the end of the day, you want to have real solutions that change things for the better.

Earlier this month one of my friends came to me with a very heartfelt confession. He's been trying to quit weed since the year began. That was his New Year's resolution because it had gotten to a point where it was a huge stress generator for him in that it was getting out of hand. He was rather addicted to doing it four times a day minimum. His first strategy was to lessen the dosage and it seemed to work, but six months in, he was sitting on my couch feeling helpless and totally freaked out.

"I mean I can manage to do it less. I'm down to just once or twice a day but I feel like the more I place emphasis on it, the more it causes me to stress out which doesn't make me feel any better. I want to embrace my empathic abilities and learn

to control and master my energy and yes smoking weed does hinder my intuitive progress, which is why I'm so anxious to quit completely, but then the entire thing overwhelms me and I end up clinging back to that daily dose. Am I just hopeless?"

If you've experienced something similar with marijuana or an addictive drug of whatever kind, my heart pours out to you. Trust that if you feel it's time to start a new chapter in your life, you will have the strength and courage to finally free yourself from that addiction.

And maybe for you, it won't be such a huge battle like it is for my friend. Perhaps it will just naturally phase itself out. However, if like him you realize it's tougher than you anticipated, don't sit and suffer alone. Get professional help, join a community that can support you and ask those you trust to help you build new rituals and triggers so you can slowly shed that old habit. You can't shame or force or punish yourself into new behavior, you must love yourself into it. Don't forget that.

Empaths and negative self-talk

Whenever something bad happens or you get into a fight (yes I know how much we hate confrontation), what's your natural impulse? Do you stoop low, feel a heavy burden come over you and literally wish you could curl up into a tiny ball and disappear? What about when someone suddenly gives you a huge compliment? Do you receive it or feel uncomfortable and unworthy of praise?

For most empaths, harsh arguments, negative situations and unpleasant environments really create a downward spiral that drops them right into the territory of self-loathing and self-judgment. It's always hard for us to spite or condemn other people, yet we do it all the time to ourselves.

Have you ever questioned why?

Negative self-talk is common in our population and everyone seems to indulge in it more than we like to admit. Researchers estimate that we think on average about 50,000 – 70,000 thoughts each day and that about 80% are negative thoughts. That's a lot of negativity.

For us as empaths, this creates a serious problem. We have to be cautious of our own negative thinking tendencies as well as avoid absorbing those of others. That's where the danger lies for us because if we're not careful, we can get affected in very powerful ways by this pervading habit.

Blaming ourselves for things that we can't control and putting ourselves down has got to stop. That's not to say you just need to shift and become a Pollyanna. Forcing yourself into positive affirmations and positive thinking like the masses promote online is barely going to work for someone as sensitive as you.

I just want you to become more self-aware. Practice being mindful of the mental temperature and the overall tone of your inner dialogue. Being more mindful will serve you better than forcing yourself to always be a positive thinker. Realize that whatever your inner dialogue sounds like will become the most dominant energy or aura around you. If you discover it's mostly dull and negative, don't stress over it for you are not stuck. You have the power to think a new thought and as you think differently and change the way you handle yourself, life will reflect back to you the same positive change.

Simply start today creating new habits and inner conversations that are more in alignment with the aura you want to walk around in. As a highly sensitive being, the last thing you want is to use those powers to tear yourself down or poison yourself with self-manufactured negativity.

Emotional eating:

Yes, this too is a habit. As much as it may seem to be out of your control, you have the power to determine your relationship with food. Gobbling down a mac and cheese or chocolate ice cream can make everything seem a little better... for a while. Overeating has this numbing effect that can help us soften the blow of unwanted energies, have you noticed?

But this can quickly escalate into an uncontrollable eating addiction that many empaths are known to fall into. Sure it can help you calm down and give you that instant distraction, a feeling of safety, security and serenity that is often elusive. A really tough, unbearable day can be soothed down quietly with some Netflix and chill with a big pint of ice cream or a dozen chocolate dementia cupcakes to help you stop feeling what you don't want to feel, but I want to encourage you to give up this coping mechanism because whether you realize it or not, this is a sign that you need to heal your relationship with food.

Emotional eating patterns are very much tied to the

mental, emotional, physical and even spiritual struggles we're dealing with. Besides, you can recall how sickly you feel afterward right?

That's why it's so important to know your triggers and create a strategy that will help you better handle the situations that cause you to overeat. In an article published on August 15th, 2017 by Harvard Health publishing, they confirm that there are parts of the brain that are rewarded from eating high-fat or high-sugar foods. And of course, we know that any behavior that is rewarded will likely be repeated. That's why researchers and experts on this topic suggest distracting yourself even if it is just for five minutes. You need to come up with creative ways that interest you to help switch gears and pour your attention into something wildly different before that automatic impulse kicks in. It could be going out for a five-minute walk, putting on your favorite song and dancing as much as you can for those three minutes or whatever else resonates with you.

As someone who understands how tough it can be to change an old habit, mine being mostly that of constant negative self-talk, I want to ensure you get something more than just airy-fairy suggestions of how to handle yourself the next time a trigger hits that you know will lead you into an old habit. The last chapter of this book is reserved purely as a resource full of practical tips to help you thrive and there's a sub-section with simple, healthy ways to soothe yourself into a calm grounded state whenever stressful situations and sensations arise. So be sure to read all the way to the end.

Alcohol and empaths:

Did you know a lot of empaths turn to alcohol to "unwind" and take the edge off as a form of self-medication?

It's common for empaths who want to numb out overwhelm and the unwanted sensations they are experiencing to resort to consumption of alcohol. And the immediate effect is actually pretty good because one does feel somewhat relaxed. The only problem is, alcohol is highly addictive. According to American Addiction Center, because alcohol is a depressant and has a sedative effect, people often use the substance to unwind. As a person's BAC rises, they often experience increased levels of relaxation. (The connection between Anxiety and Alcohol November 2018)

Most of the time it does feel great to mask the

underlying problems we're faced with and temporarily relieve ourselves of the suffocating effects that are often associated with being an empath, but when this starts to backfire (and trust me it will) the consequences can be devastating.

I recently came across a blogger who is sharing how he's been drinking from the age of six to help get rid of the angst and discomfort that accompanied him whenever his parents dragged him into one of the many social gatherings. They are complete extroverts and always seemed to enjoy being in large crowds. It was a nightmare for him; they just thought he was being "too emotional" and in the end, since he couldn't get out of it, his way of coping became sneaking in a drink or two. He called it "his miracle drug" because in just a few shots he could quickly drive away the depression, anxiety, paranoia and overwhelm he was experiencing. It was his ticket to freedom.

But you and I both know this type of freedom is always very temporary. It took him 20 years of frequent alcohol intake (which eventually turned into a daily routine) to hit rock bottom and realize he's become his own worst nightmare. Alcohol worked until it didn't work anymore. And at 26yrs old, his body and mind refused to cooperate any longer. It was time to either make a change and save his life before it was too late or simply call it quits. I don't know how his journey is currently progressing but with the support of online readers who are probably walking the same path, I am certain he will find a way to overcome the addiction.

The point for us to drill home is that alcoholism never ends well. Sure it gives that false sense of freedom and control, but what happens the next further down the road?

I know it has become a tool for survival for many empaths and sure, drinking is one way to improve your mood and escape anxiety for a time, but it's also the fastest way to imprison yourself, paralyze your future and bring about a lot of pain and grief to those closest to you.

Now I know what you might be thinking...

Could a little alcohol be okay?

Surely one or two glasses a day isn't too bad. Well, that's still debatable. A new scientific study concludes there is no safe level of drinking alcohol. The International Medical Journal *The Lancet*, made headlines when they showed that in 2016, nearly 3 million deaths globally were attributed to alcohol use including 12% of deaths in males between the ages of 14 - 49. (New scientific study: no safe level of alcohol August 2018)

Whether or not you choose to make alcohol your "miracle medicine" is a choice only you can make. No one can tell you whether or not you can safely handle any amount of alcohol, because only you know how it feels once you ingest that first glass of wine or beer. Be conscious about your choice to drink alcohol and let that decision be based on how you want to show up in the world.

Procrastination:

Sometimes it gets hard to cope with everyday tasks as an empath, especially when we haven't fully owned our empathic abilities. To outsiders, you might just seem like a lazy passive and spaced-out person and I think that's one of the reasons why empaths struggle to transform this unhealthy habit. They often feel alone, misunderstood and stuck with no one to come to their aid.

Procrastination doesn't just affect empaths. In fact, it is such a common habit even Ellen DeGeneres talked about it in her stand up comedy show.

Procrastination is when we put off making a decision or we avoid taking some form of action and usually for empaths, it's a coping mechanism.

Lynda Williams shares how procrastination has been a monster in her life, especially when dealing with depression. "*It's easy to assume that people like me who procrastinate are lazy; the truth is, if I could do it now, I would,*" she says with tears rolling down her cheeks.

I think this is something we can all relate to at some level. And I have been caught in that awful cycle where I shame and guilt myself which only makes me feel worse and I still don't get done what I know needs to get done. I mean even today, with all the knowledge, tools and living strategies that I use to empower myself I still have to deal with procrastination from time to time.

Procrastination hits an all-time high for empaths when we are specifically going through a bad spell. If there's too much overwhelm, anxiety or depression it's a lot easier to procrastinate. I think it's because when our energy is low, it's just not possible to sell yourself into being productive and doing even something as silly as washing dishes. So you just let them sit there and pile up. And the more they pile up, the worse we feel which of course creates this cycle of doom and self-manufactured loathing.

Now before you stamp off this unhealthy habit as beyond our control (especially when we are going through tough times), it's important to remember that procrastination is rooted in fear.

When the energy of fear is tuned up within you whether that originated from you or someone else, your tendency to procrastinate is activated and soon after a feeling of guilt, shame and self-remorse which then builds this new momentum. After a while, you won't even remember where this thing generated from and trying to force yourself out of that funk may not work. So rather than beating yourself up or forcing yourself to do something when you're clearly not up to it, step back from the situation and give yourself permission to just be.

Take a nap if you have to and break that momentum first. Then remind yourself that fear is usually the energy culprit fueling this habit. So work on clearing your energy first and foremost before stepping back into the chores or goals you wish to accomplish.

EMBRACING THE EMPATH EXPERIENCE

"Before healing others, heal yourself."
- Gambian saying

This feels like an opportune time to dive a little deeper into the empath experience and what it feels like to go through life feeling everything.

I think it's important to always remember that every human being experiences varying degrees of empathy unless there's a particular discord within them that creates a block.

And life is tough for a lot of people. Finding peace and happiness is not easy in our modern world even for those who don't consider themselves empathic.

Social media and news are great at amplifying the negative side of humanity, which only makes our interactions with others all the more challenging. What we must do is figure out the aspects that we have control over as we go through daily interactions and work on enhancing them.

Therefore the empath experience isn't about making you feel like an alien from another planet. There's nothing wrong with how you experience this human journey. Just because people around you interact with life and interpret things at a different level from you doesn't make your high sensitivities good or bad. It just means your senses are refined. You are tuned in to the dance of life at an unusual level and the best way to enjoy this dance is to figure out the best way you can make the most of it.

Living on a planet with eight Billion fellow humans is a bit crowded for an empath, but we are here for a reason. It's not an accident that you were given this gift and the best use of it would be in service to yourself and others.

While I know how tough public places, crowded malls, and large gatherings can be, I still believe it's possible to find the balance that enables you to interact with the world in ways that are comfortable and reassuring for you.

We know that as empaths walking into a room, a grocery store, a company meeting, a restaurant and even flying with other people can be a very overwhelming experience. As a matter of fact I was recently on a short two hour flight and due to the fact that I hadn't slept my optimum eight hours sleep all week, my mind was a little bit hazy and I was having a hard time controlling my energies as per usual. I sat down, buckled up and rather than jump right into a book I decided to simply observe what others around me were doing. It was a morning flight, my eyes were really feeling the distress of sleeping so little and I didn't feel like listening to music. So my attention landed on a group of young rowdy guys probably from Russia who were obviously excited about being on a plane. The four of them caused quite a bit of ruckus coming in and one of them had a tough time even paying attention to the instructions of the flight attendant. I couldn't tell if he was just being stubborn or trying to flirt with her.

Either way, he was getting on her nerves and I slowly started experiencing the same angst and irritation she was feeling. She also seemed to be struggling with a sore throat and the more I paid attention to this situation, the more I started feeling my throat tingle. I quickly caught myself absorbing the energy from the flight attendant and took the necessary precaution to filter it through. Having learned from past experiences where I would catch someone's anger or headache or some other symptom I never let myself get too carried away even on my "hazy days". The point I'm trying to make is we can get overwhelmed and absorbed into other energies really fast.

The vibes and emotional sensations being broadcasted from our surroundings are always real and vivid to us. It's no wonder we try to escape it all by any means necessary. Most of the time, the escape routes we choose end up hurting us far more, whether that be overeating, smoking, alcohol drug or some other addiction.

I'm not here to make light of the daily struggle you face trying to fit into a society that isn't very welcoming to our kind. As a matter of fact, I don't want you to fit into the status quo at all. That would destroy you.

What I do want is for you to become proactive with

your lifestyle choices and the framework for living that you establish.

If for example like my friend you've ended up abandoning a shopping cart in the middle of a supermarket because of how overwhelming things got during your Christmas shopping spree, rather than completely cut out shopping from your life, get more strategic with the timings when you choose to go shopping. Find out those times when crowds of people aren't storming in and enjoy doing your shopping in solace. You will still be exposed to the different energies of the staff, the few patrons who, like you, would rather shop in peace and quiet and you'll have more "breathing space" to interact with the energy of the food you purchase.

Public places do not need to be torturous if you create strong frameworks for living and a few tactics for engaging publicly at your own chosen time.

Some empaths find it unbearable to experience daily human living under normal social conditions so they lock themselves away somewhere. They either move out of big cities into secluded farms or hardly ever leave their city apartment unless absolutely necessary.

I can only speak from personal experience when I say this. My conviction is that total isolation isn't the answer to happiness, peace of mind and freedom for an empath. It is true we need solitude and frequent time alone but totally isolating ourselves as a result of fear or overwhelm means we end up settling for a very limited lifestyle. It is impossible to thrive when held captive to such limiting beliefs and emotions.

As we interact and respond to the world fully in our power, I believe it becomes essential to master the art of simply becoming aware of other people's energies and accepting them just as they are. In other words, I want you to train yourself to go out into the world, grounded in your own power, open to sensing emotions and vibes from others and rather than trying to fight them off or fix them, just observe and filter them out. Those you wish to absorb remain with you and those that do not fit you simply flow back to their source.

I believe you have a choice to make as you continue reading this book. You can continue accepting a life of victimhood. Where even your own life doesn't feel like it's truly yours and any interaction feels stressful because you're always anxious about taking in more than is good for you.

Or... You can choose to liberate yourself and abilities.

There are many practical things you can do immediately and I share some of these practical tips in the last chapter. I will also be sharing with you some of the benefits of embracing the empathic experiences in an upcoming chapter, because I want you to see all the good you can do once you fully own and master your powers. In so doing you become an empowered empath who not only thrives but also heals the world in the process.

6

EMPATHS AND RELATIONSHIPS

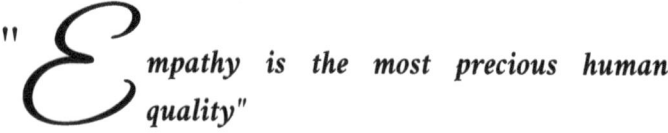
"Empathy is the most precious human quality"

- Dalai Lama

Dealing with relationships as an empath is a big challenge. I'm sure you know what I mean. Whether it's professional, intimate or family relationships. We love being deeply connected to others and sharing meaningful experiences but creating such relationships in our modern world is easier said than done.

We are highly creative, thoughtful, intuitive, super passionate individuals and the excitement we bring to any relationship when properly understood is one to be savored. However, it is true there are lots of challenges to be faced as we attempt to create rich nourishing relationships that empower us. Majority of the people around us don't "feel" or process things as deeply as we do and that can be very challenging to deal with.

So despite the fact that we too desire that chance to experience true love with a soul mate or nurture enriching relationships with the people we care about, our approach to love and all kinds of relationships needs to be somewhat unique given our highly sensitive nature. The struggle is real and we've had to endure it for a long time. It's time to turn a new leaf.

Why you've been struggling with romance

Because we feel everything so intensely, being in love as an empath is out of this world. And I mean this in the positive and negative. When you find that right match, being madly in love and intensely passionate are a norm. The exchange of energy is incredible and you tend to be very addicting for your partner. This can be an amazing experience for both of you.

However, if you end up with a match that isn't right

for you the same energetic exchange will have a huge negative impact. This is probably why most empaths avoid intimacy. Once you've burned a few times from choosing poorly, your entire being refuses to go down that dark path again.

The other issue is the fact that being moody often plays out when we get romantically involved. Because all our emotions be they joy, anger, sadness or happiness are so heightened, sometimes they get out of control. What's worse is when you absorb the feelings of someone else while out and about with your partner that creates a completely different outcome for the two of you.

Do you find yourself totally excited about starting a relationship only to feel burdened and freaked out a few months in?

This is mostly due to the fact that as empaths, we don't take the time to set healthy boundaries and fully express our sensitivities and dislikes to our new partner. If the person you're in a relationship with is right for you, they will understand and appreciate the fact that you regularly need space and alone time.

They will not impose their beliefs on you or

compare your relationship with other people. The issue has never been your inability to be a good partner; it's about being romantically involved with someone who helps you emerge as the best version of yourself.

It's nearly impossible for us to hide our feelings and being that vulnerable usually complicates things unless you have someone just like you or at least understands your nature. In our modern society where authenticity and genuine compassion, affection, and attention are a rare commodity, romance is a tough one for us. Superficial dating is the trend. We can't stand anything that isn't authentic.

Showing off, trying to gather as much attention as possible especially on social media is what "cool" couples do. That stuff totally turns us off.

How to handle intimate relationships as an empath

We all want to have meaningful relationships whether it's with a friend, a family member, co-worker and especially those we fall madly in love with. Yet finding that special someone who is both your soul mate and best friend is no easy feat for empaths. The best way to cultivate and nurture an intimate relationship when you feel you've found the right person is by using your special abilities to form a healthy bond.

Notice I say healthy bond.

Not just any bond. Your connection needs to run deep. Far deeper than the superficial level at which most people run their relationships. Because by default you're finely tuned to higher perceptions, you need to be with someone who can connect with you at that level too.

This is where science and spirituality crossfade into each other.

An intimate relationship that doesn't connect the two of you physically, mentally, emotionally and spiritually will have a hard time lasting or satisfying you.

When I say spiritual connection, I'm not talking about a religious thing unless that's your preference. I simply mean you need to create a bond that is grounded in something deeper; it doesn't need to be religious or even spiritual (as defined by social norms). Depending on both your beliefs it can be whatever grounds and empowers both of you.

In essence, what you want to do is create a container for being holistically connected and vulnerable with each other. Where both of you pour in the best versions of yourselves until you develop this inner knowing that no matter what, your partner will be that empowering force for good in your life and vice-versa.

Couples with similar interests and viewpoints are better able to form this type of bond. It helps them develop habits and rituals that strengthen their bond and becomes a foundation for their relationship that can weather any storm.

As an empath, you know expressing your emotions come naturally and when you're in love it's almost magical. The best way to ensure these experiences turn into a lifetime of joy and meaningful experiences for you is by working on yourself so that you can easily match yourself up with someone worthy of enjoying this passionate ride of intimacy.

Settling for anything less than that special someone who lights you up is a big no-no. To help you with that, here are four tips for building a healthy intimate relationship and strong connection with your chosen partner.

1. Identify the primary intention of why you want to be in this relationship.

When you enter into a relationship with someone, don't do it blindly. Because the moment you start, it's as though the relationship becomes a third entity with its own frequency. Have you noticed?

Most people don't even realize this. But being the highly sensitive person you are, you've probably had moments where you could definitely tell there was a third energy in the room.

Usually, after a few months of being together it becomes more palpable since, in many instances, routine kicks in and momentum slows down. So you might even start to experience some heavy or dull energy that is neither yours nor your beloved's. This is because energy flows where attention goes. If one or both of you stop paying attention to the nurturing of your relationship and instead life's obligations distract you, the energy of the relationships stagnates.

For an empath, this becomes a major issue. Our less empathic counterparts would hardly pick up on this until things physically spiral out of control, but for us, we sense it immediately.

Which is why it's so important to get clear on why you're in the relationship in the first place. Go into it with clarity and powerful intentions. Discuss your intentions with your partner and make sure you're both on the same page.

2. Self-reflect as often as possible.

Whether you are looking to attract into your life someone special or have already entered into a relationship, nothing is more important than taking the time to find out who you really are. The more you can continuously be in your body, present, fully aware and grounded in your own power the more enjoyable your intimate relationship becomes. That strong bond with another can only take place when you know who you are and what you desire.

Take a private journal now and jot down some thoughts to the following questions:

- What are your viewpoints on religion and spirituality?

- What does intimacy mean to you?

- How do you best like to express your love?

- How do you best like to receive love?

- How do you define romance?

- What are your core values?

- What are your viewpoints on religion and spirituality?

- What would you love to experience with your soul mate?

- What are some of your main desires? Why do they matter to you and how do you stay connected and true to them?

- Do you have daily rituals and practices that keep you grounded such as meditation, prayer, devotion etc.?

- Do you enjoy having higher consciousness conversations with someone you're in a relationship with? What about sexual explorations?

3. Prioritize meaningful conversations that openly express intimacy and affection.

Now that you've had some time to self-reflect and contemplate what matters to you, it's time to include the love of your life. Even if you're just dating and it's not yet something serious, openly have this conversation with your beloved.

Share with them your viewpoints and give them the chance to open up as well and share where they stand. Finding out what's important to him or her right off the bat is actually a great way to start building that strong foundation and bond.

It also helps you realize sooner rather than later whether you two are traveling on the same path or if you're willing to step onto the same path together.

4. Give yourself space and downtime needed to manage your own energy.

As you establish this open communication with your partner and they get to fully understand how special you are, one of the things you'll both need to agree on is creating that downtime and space necessary to help you reset regularly.

Aside from designing little practices that help you build a strong bond and express greater affection, giving you that solitude that every empath needs should be prioritized. If your partner is empathic as well, they too will benefit greatly from this agreement but even if they aren't, I believe anyone who truly loves you will understand and help you create a lifestyle that offers you greater joy and freedom.

Love is the most powerful force in our universe and

we know how to flow it passionately better than most. We must stop being afraid of freely offering our love and getting intimate with the right person. Of course, the caveat is "offering it to the right person".

So far, I have shared ways for you to be more open to intimacy and how to maintain a healthy relationship with the right partner. But we all know there are too many horrid stories of empaths who find themselves stuck in toxic relationships that feel like hell on earth. If you've been in such a relationship, you know how suffocating that can be. And it can certainly have very negative consequences, especially on your health. So before moving on to the next chapter where we'll work on helping you thrive at work, let's touch on ways you can protect or free yourself from unhealthy relationships.

Protecting yourself from toxic relationships

Here are a few quickie tips to protect you from harmful relationships.

1. Re-evaluate your principles and core values:

The number one reason to enter into any relationship is that it makes you feel happier and brings out the best in you. Period. Which means your top values need to be aligned and activated within that relationship. So if for example, a core value is freedom, getting into a relationship with a control freak won't work no matter how smitten you are.

It's a very good idea to sit and consciously make a list of your core values and the principles by which to run your life. Then just underneath create another list of what I call "deal breakers". This is essentially a list of the qualities you most treasure in a partner and without these, you just won't settle.

These are often qualities such as gentle, free-spirited, good listener etc. Be sure though that this list is a reflection of the core values you possess and that you too are displaying the same qualities you seek in your partner. You can only attract what you are not what you say you want.

2. Raise your personal standards:

Because empaths are so attractive and can get anyone (even total strangers) to open up and share their feelings, it can be tricky knowing when to pull the plug on a budding relationship.

Oftentimes it's just so easy to get into one we may not take the time to consciously determine whether it's actually good for us. That's why raising your standards is so vital. Your intimate relationships need to meet certain criterion, which you determine. It can't just be anyone's game.

You are extremely valuable as a person. You're super passionate, gifted and honestly, one of the best lovers anyone could have, so why just let anyone wiggle themselves into your private world? The higher you raise the bar when it comes to intimate relationships and close friendships, the harder it becomes for anything less than what you truly desire and deserve to successfully push its way through into your world.

3. Let the past go. Do you find that your past keeps sneaking up on you?

Like every time you date someone you quickly realize they have the same negative traits that your parents had? If so, then you have what Freud called repetition compulsion. It could be a childhood condition that makes you feel like you deserve this "bad experience" because that's what you were raised with so in your mind it's "normal" for people to be condescending or mistreat you. But that's not true.

I'm here to tell you it is time to let go of your past. You are not your past failures or your parent's limitations. How others have treated you or reacted to you in the past has nothing to do with who you are and it's about time to release the old and embrace a new you.

5. Work on your sense of deservability.

Have you spent your whole life struggling with feelings of unworthiness? Do you often have voices in your head asking, *"Who are you to be loved deeply?"*

It's very challenging to live a fulfilled life and find someone who will love you for all that you are when you silently doubt how much you deserve it. I know your background, society and past experience may have created lots of tension in your mind about what you deserve to experience in this life, but I strongly urge you to question those beliefs. You need to know and believe that you deserve a good life, a safe space to live and work. And you must believe that you deserve to be loved because you are loveable.

The more confident and deserving you feel about being loved by someone wonderful, the easier it will be to only match up with a partner that will enhance your life. It's very simple really, what you believe you deserve is what you will attract from others so work on this as much as possible.

6. Practice self-love.

Sure you've seen and heard this concept everywhere online. But do you really practice it? If you're always keenly aware of how awful your body, career or sensitivities are, it's highly unlikely you'll find anyone who can truly love you.

Most of us are so giving and loving to others yet we can barely look at ourselves straight in the mirror after a shower without feeling shame disgust or self-loathing.

In order to be loveable, you must first love yourself. Love is all around you but in order for you to experience more of it, you must be giving from a place of wholeness and self-acceptance.

7. Set clear intentions and a positive energetic shield around yourself.

I'm not entirely convinced that building protective shields actually leads to a happier, prosperous life for empaths. But what I do know is that we work with energy. As such, we can be more intentional about the dominant energy that we emanate at any given moment. If you train yourself to be expansive and strongly concentrated with passionate, powerful and highly positive energy, by the universal law of cause and effect, you can only produce effects that correspond to that cause.

So rather than worry too much about building protective shields that keep toxic people out, focus on becoming a source of powerful positive energy that encapsulates your entire being as you go through daily human interactions and watch how different things become for you.

As an empath, you have special needs and it's important to honor yours and communicate them to the people you're in a relationship with. There are many wonderful strategies and practical tips that you will be getting at the end of the book to really equip you with the solutions that will lead to a holistic thriving lifestyle. Now you feel a little more equipped to deal with all kinds of relationships, don't you? Let's keep going.

EMPATHS AND WORK

"*My feeling is we need more compassion, we need more empathy, and we need more togetherness, in terms of working together.*"

- Cindy McCain

According to Harvard Health Publishing, there is an overlooked issue in the workplace where employees are silently struggling with some form of mental illness yet no one wants to address it.

"Researchers analyzing results from the U.S National Comorbidity Survey, a nationally representative study of Americans ages 15 to 54 reported that 18% of those who were employed said they experience symptoms of a mental disorder in the previous month." ("Mental health problems in the workplace, February 2010")

A similar survey was done by mental health charity, Mind in the U.K where more than 44,000employees were surveyed and 48% of all people who participated said they experienced a mental health problem in their current job. And of that 48 %, only half of those people struggling with this experience ever talked to their employer about it. So basically we are looking at one in four U.K workers silently struggling in the workplace. I bet if we check in other countries as well, we would find a lot of people who are going to work every morning and hating every minute of it.

Are you currently experiencing a similar issue? Are you feeling so drained, burnt out and misunderstood in the workplace that quitting seems like the only option? Or perhaps you've previously quit in frustration only to land another job or start a new business that later on became burdensome. Because you are an empath, the work experience will definitely require you to approach things differently if you want to thrive and live well.

I know many empaths are told they need to take up jobs that are more intuitive, spiritual and healing in nature such as therapy or other "helping" professions but here's the thing. The main reason work becomes a struggle and at times a nightmare is because of the energy battles and emotional conflicts you keep facing.

Meaning, it's all about your energy and how you're protecting it. If you're absorbing so much negative energy in your environment and succumbing to its ill effects, switching to a different job, career or business may not be the best answer. So before giving up hope about your current work situation and feeling doomed, let's review some key insights that I feel will help protect and nourish your empathic abilities in the workplace.

How to approach your work and career

It's very simple really. Your heart must be in line with the work that you do in order to thrive as an empath. Forget about what loud-mouthed motivators, marketers, and cynics of this world say, this is the best time in human history to be alive. You know why?

You can control your own destiny.

Never has it been more feasible and easier for anyone, anywhere to create the quality of life they desire. It doesn't really matter what your vocation is, as long as you build a strong foundation around it, you will succeed.

The way you approach your work or job, as an empath ought to be the same way you approach everything else in life. You and I both know compartmentalizing doesn't work for empaths. Why put yourself through the trauma that comes from trying to settle for work that doesn't align with your core values and sensitivities?

Remember the exercise we did for attracting better relationships? I encourage you to do the same for your work. Approach it like you would meeting a soul mate and make a list of all the qualities, experiences and criterion you wish your work life to embody. It doesn't matter whether you're an entrepreneur serving clients or an employee with a boss, colleagues, and clients to think of. It is the intention you set and the grounding foundations you establish that will determine how much you can enjoy your work-life.

Generally, empaths are drawn to mission-driven, meaningful work that makes a difference in the world. Because you know this to be true of you, do everything you can to align with opportunities that reflect this truth.

However, don't fall for the misconception that it means you must become a spiritual healer, psychic medium, coach or any of the various helping professions associated with empathic abilities.

I know empaths who are engineers, managers, entrepreneurs, doctors, and even investment bankers. There is no limit to the contribution you can make to the world with your gifts and you need never limit yourself to thinking that only artists and healers get to build careers using their empathic abilities. If anything, I believe the more you become empowered as an empath, the more helpful you will be in areas like HR and senior management positions where people are really feeling unappreciated. But you cannot help or give if you're still overwhelmed, uncontrolled and unstable in your own power. As that Gambian saying reveals, we must first heal ourselves before extending out to help others.

You need to gain full understanding and control of your sensitivities and use it in positive powerful ways.

The more you understand energy and the way it works, the easier it will be to make smart choices on your job role.

Contrary to popular belief, you don't have to choose between making money and helping people. And you certainly don't have to pretend to be something you're not just to fit into a work environment. When you compromise who you really are, you can never do your best work. So rather than approaching your work from the viewpoint of "trying to fit in", I invite you to figure out what your strengths are, the contribution you want to make to our global economy and the gifts and skills you want to develop that align with your empathic powers. From there, choose the vocation that best ticks all those boxes.

Lynn Taylor, a national workplace expert and author of *Tame Your Terrible Office Tyrant; How to Manage Childish Boss Behavior and Thrive in Your Job* says, "people want to connect on a humane level in the office; the alternative is a sterile environment with low productivity. So, the more you demonstrate these abilities, the faster your career will advance. It's the 'office diplomats' with strong emotional intelligence who are most likely to be strong, effective corporate leaders. They realize that trusting relationships built on diplomacy and respect are at the heart of both individual success and corporate productivity. An ounce of people sensitivity is worth a pound of cure when it comes to daily human interaction and mitigating conflict. By developing these skills, you'll reduce bad behavior in the office and your positive approach will be contagious."

An ounce of your sensitivities is worth a pound of cure in today's business world.

This to me is the free pass empaths have been waiting for. It's the confirmation that the workplace is shifting in a major way. Business is getting a makeover. Authenticity is now one of the major things customers demand. Empowerment, empathy and genuine connection are what every employee craves. And everyone is now recognizing that empowered empaths are valuable members in the workplace. Your time to flourish as an empowered empath has come provided you do the groundwork within yourself.

Feeling safe and empowered at work

Chances are, the more you feel empowered, valued and appreciated for your abilities, the more satisfied and fulfilled you will be with your chosen vocation. I'm giving you permission right here and now to stop exhausting yourself and applying strenuous effort to fit into a work environment that does not suit you.

By now you're well aware that when certain things are in your immediate working environment, you don't perform at your best. Anxiety jumps in and takes over very quickly for empaths, so we need to make sure you set parameters that help reduce or eliminate anxiety triggers.

<u>One</u>: Excessive sounds, lights or continuous inter-personal interaction from co-workers can become a drain for us and cause us to feel really exhausted.

Helpful hint:

Consider taking a personal initiative to create a safe environment for yourself around the workplace. For example, if you have to work in a place with lots of noise and there's no possible option to get moved somewhere quiet, invest in a headset piece that cuts out all noise.

What are some other small creative things you can do to improve your immediate work environment?

Two: Decluttering your workspace and always ensuring it's clean is actually super important. And you can't leave it to the company to take care of it whether they pay a great cleaning team or not.

The decorations, sense of ease and organization around your desk are your responsibility and it does affect you because your energy is immersed in that state for several hours each day.

Many empaths and highly sensitive people report feeling unsettled in cluttered environments. There's simply too much sensory information to process.

Helpful Hint:

Consider going for a minimalist set up in your work environment. Declutter your office or workspace regularly and create a sensation of relaxation, openness, and calmness as much as you can.

Three: Work on simplifying that complex inner dialogue that makes you feel it's not okay to be sensitive and aware of other people's emotions at work.

As you have learned thus far, not only is it a beautiful thing that you possess empathic abilities, even the workplace is slowly shifting to the understanding that leaders with your qualities might be the best way forward. This means the more you can tame your wild inner dialogue and shift your old beliefs to perceiving yourself as a powerful, valued force for good, the easier it will be for others to receive that broadcast and reflect it back to you.

Helpful Hint:

Regardless of where you work or travel to in this world, a true feeling of safety, peace, and empowerment can only be born from within. There will never be someone from the outside who comes and solves your issues. You are the only one who can train your mind into positive constructive thinking. Learn to perceive yourself as strong, powerful, safe and secure.

To seek security from the outside world is a temporary solution that will keep backfiring on you. So what do you think it would take for you to develop an inner dialogue of safety, security, and empowerment today?

Four: Trying to please everyone or going out of your way just to avoid conflict even if it means absorbing and holding on to that negative energy will never be a good long-term strategy if you want to thrive as an empath.

I mean think about it, whether you're employed, a freelancer or a business owner you will always be dealing with people. And there are good and bad people no matter where you look. You could just as easily find a boss or customer that is tough to deal with.

Helpful Hint:

Establish a healthier way (that resonates with your personality) to deal with such situations. Using verbal Aikido for example might be a great option to consider.

Five: Aggression in the workplace is often acceptable for our less empathic counterparts but we know how harmful it can be for us. It's important you never allow your energy to get sucked into the whirlpool that aggressive colleagues and even customers enjoy because, to me, those who are always stirring up arguments, tantrums and verbally attacking others are merely projecting their insecurities. Don't fall into that trap.

Helpful Hint:

Ever heard of verbal Aikido? This is the perfect time to practice it. Aikido is a modern Japanese martial art created by a martial arts master named Morihei Ueshiba. The fundamental principle underlying this martial arts is that during any conflict we should always seek to neutralize, not harm, the opponent.

In practicing this, we would be applying the underlying philosophy of personal evolution in the context of dealing with the verbal and energetic exchange. It would require us to integrate all our sensitivities and practice mental, emotional and spiritual self-control to our communication. I'm not saying it's easy to do or that you'll get it right the first time, but if you're tired of running, hiding and absorbing conflict like a powerless victim, it's worth a try. Like any technique, the more you learn and practice it, the greater the benefits.

Finding work that works for you

Now that you are beginning to see that the working world isn't meant to be a hostile torturous place for you, how about we figure out what work will give you that sense of fulfillment and satisfaction.

As Einstein once said, the most important question you can ever ask yourself is, Is this a friendly universe? If your answer is yes, then surely this universe wants you to enjoy full expression of your skills and natural gifts in every way possible including your work life. I believe we are all here for something meaningful and it is our duty to find out what we can be and do on planet earth that brings meaning to others and ourselves. If this is how you view your work life, you can't go wrong. The question is where do you begin?

Make the most of your sensitivities.

Rather than treating your empathic abilities as some kind of a mistake that makes you a misfit in society, think of them as the superpowers that make you instantly unique. In truth, I believe that's exactly what they are.

That doesn't mean you are better or more special than other individuals, it just means these are the gifts you were given to explore, work with and eventually utilize for the highest good of all people.

Judith Orloff M.D also believes that as an empath, we can only excel and enjoy our work when we express our intuition, thoughtfulness, quietness, and creativity. She presents the pros and cons of certain careers and working conditions based on her experience and feels that empaths do better in lower stress environments, solo jobs or with small companies. She also says that many of her patients prefer being self-employed to avoid drain and overwhelm from coworkers, bosses and packed schedules. But here's the thing. It's not a standard rule. As I mentioned before, I know empaths that are engineers and doctors running a tight schedule and receiving amazing recognition for their work.

So giving you a linear answer to such a complex topic that is purely relative to the individual wouldn't be fair to your growth and progress. What I can tell you is this. You don't have to be a writer, health care professional, musician, graphics designer, animal rescuer, psychotherapist or a life coach to thrive as an empath. In fact, if you're not doing work that enables you to demonstrate the highest expression of your truest Self, even a seemingly empathic profession like healing others can drain and overwhelm you.

I have a Spanish friend who used to be a card reader and energy healer. But she was always sick, felt lonely and could never make enough money to pay her monthly bills. We first met at a Starbucks coffee shop where I was sitting busily typing on my computer and she was frantically moving up and down in search of a power plug to charge her dying phone.

When I noticed she was struggling to get anyone to share with her their spot, I offered up mine and asked her to sit and join me while her phone recharged. That became the beginning of a very heartfelt conversation where I learned all about her struggles and gifts. I quickly realized she was an empath. She had never heard of this term but it made complete sense to her. After hearing how unhappy she was despite the joy she felt when someone got healed during her treatments, I encouraged her to really contemplate her underlying beliefs. What she needed was a paradigm shift. The same paradigm shift you'll be experiencing on the next chapter. Six months after we became friends, she was working in a retirement home fulltime and her health had greatly improved. Now she's working on tapping into that right frequency of a loving soul mate and you know what? I have no doubt in my mind she's just about to bump into him.

I've come across many life coaches, therapists and healers who need more help than the patients they are trying to heal. And I have also come across life coaches and energy healers with profitable businesses.

Bottom line?

The work that enables you to express the best and highest version of yourself while integrating your empathic abilities is the only work you should be going after. Your skills, temperament, and gifts are valuable to all kinds of careers. So just use your intuition when considering a job or business to go into. Make sure in your gut and in your body it feels right and that you resonate with the space, people, energy and environment you want to serve.

This is by far the best way to take care of your energy and enhance your empathic abilities. It will also reduce the risk of constantly being drained and fatigued at work. Here's just a short list of jobs experts on this topic recommend you avoid and those they suggest you consider. If none of them feels right, do a little more research online based on your skills, talent, and passion and simply choose to bet on yourself.

Jobs to avoid:

Politics.

Attorney.

Executive manager for large corporations.

Used car salesman.

A cashier at big store chains.

Policeman or Policewoman.

Fire fighter.

Public relations.

Jobs to consider:

Veterinary.

Massage therapist.

Working at an animal shelter or animal rescue.

An employee at a non-profit organization.

Hospice worker.

Social worker.

Psychotherapist.

Chinese medical practitioners.

THE GIFT OF BEING AN EMPATH

"*The higher your energy level, the more efficient your body. The more efficient your body, the better you feel and the more you will use your talent to produce outstanding results.*"

- *Tony Robbins.*

At this point in our journey together it must be clear to you that I am a strong advocate for owning your empathic abilities and proudly showing them to the world.

Yes, there's the challenge that comes with that given how rigid and impervious our society has become. A big portion of our global population sits on the middle to the extreme opposite end spectrum of the empathy scale, where they've made it seem like it's normal to "feel nothing". So on those times when it feels really hard embracing your unique abilities, step back from the heat of the moment and ground yourself in the truth.

What truth?

This is a journey and you will go through different stages that will move you from that state of feeling burdened by your gifts to feeling fully empowered. Oftentimes you will come across people who are also going through their tests, trials and tribulations and depending on their level of awareness, they may or may not appreciate you for who you really are. There's nothing wrong with that; learn to see the value in everyone's point of view without compromising yours.

You are a unique individual; a piece of life itself made to perfection. Everything you possess is there not by accident, but by design. Including your empathic abilities. On the empathy spectrum, you sit high up on that scale where it's not just about being a highly sensitive person, it's about being a gifted person who can perceive and interpret life with incredible detail.

This is a very good thing. Your heightened level of awareness must never be shut down, muted off or hidden from the world. You need a constant reminder telling you that you are a valuable member of our world. That you are more than good enough. The wonderful traits you possess set you apart and give you the advantage you need to design your dream lifestyle.

Take a deep breath in, repeat that sentence again if you need to and just soak in it for a moment.

I am a valuable member of my community. I am more than good enough and where I am now is the right place and the right time for me to start shining.

Receive this knowing and live from it starting now.

The paradigm shift that gives you the freedom to be an empath.

Let me set the stage here by warning you beforehand that you may not fully agree with this section of the book and that's okay. However, don't back out from reading it with an open mind and heart as you never know what may come of it.

Most of the information we have on the Internet around empaths, the struggle of dealing with the world and the dangers of falling for narcissists and energy vampires tend to be very one-sided. There is a tendency to make it seem as though it's out of our control as empaths. What we fail to openly discuss is the fact that there are underlying beliefs that shape all our realities. When those beliefs are detrimental to our wellbeing, it becomes a self-fulfilling prophecy whereby we produce conditions, situations, and experiences corresponding to said beliefs.

In order for us to grow as human beings and especially as empaths, we must gather enough courage and confront the lies that we often tell ourselves.

What we find in the world is a reflection of our underlying paradigms.

Yes, this is a tough one to swallow, but it is true nonetheless. The tendency to get into relationships or situations that make you a pathological giver is actually rooted in a negative belief system active within you.

Your willingness to self-sacrifice, the insecurities, self-doubt and other negative thought patterns are what make you a perfect prey for narcissists and other energy vampires. So one of the major paradigm shifts you need to boldly address is the active belief that your needs are illegitimate, less worthy and that you're undeserving of having the best in life.

Because of your highly sensitive nature and depending on your upbringing, you could be running on a belief system that was conditioned during your formative years to perceive yourself as a burden and someone who is weak and too passive. If that's the case then emotions like resentment, anger, pain even loneliness could be buried deep within and project themselves in your life in the most unusual ways.

Let me give you another example of my Spanish friend. She had been married once to a man she could only describe as a sadistic control freak. He not only mistreated her during their marriage, but also made sure he left her feeling worthless and undeserving of ever being loved the day he ran off with another woman.

When she started working on herself and the story of her former husband came up, she was still emotionally tormented by the entire experience. It was as if he was still alive in her controlling her emotions.

She felt small and insignificant. Her entire energy would shift as soon as she started talking about him. She wanted to remarry and fall in love of course, but the truth is, she was better off being on her own, until she figured out the limiting beliefs that ruled her mind. Working on herself and building a new paradigm was the prudent thing to do before attempting to call in another relationship.

The mere fact that three years after he left she was still feeling like the betrayed victim full of resentment, hurt and anger for having given him too much was exactly why I told her to work on shifting her paradigm first. The issue isn't who was right or wrong. Here is a classic case of an empath that never realizes the underlying belief system that causes such conditions to manifest in her life. I want you to free yourself from that same trap if you recognize a pattern with your current work or relationships.

Victim mentality is a very twisted and complex belief system to possess and will require some effort from your end to even become aware of what's going on underneath. Due to the fact that you have access to the emotions of everyone around you, it's all too easy to get yourself entangled and completely lose access to the depth of your own beliefs. That's why your freedom begins with becoming aware of the long-held belief system and shifting it accordingly.

Take a moment now to become aware of what you really believe about yourself. And I don't mean the surface level affirmations or things you say to others. Take a look at yourself in the mirror and go as deep as you can.

Taking back your power

It goes without saying that most of what messes you up and keeps you from being your best self are underlying beliefs from childhood that just don't fit into a healthy, prosperous adult lifestyle.

You need to be courage and boldness. Face your own darkened energies and start healing those aspects of you that clearly demonstrate these underlying negative beliefs. Your state of consciousness and the beliefs you hold are projected outwardly in the people you meet, the quality of life you have and the happiness your experience. Therefore taking your power back is a matter of learning how to retrain your mind and getting more control over your energies so that you can establish new parameters and belief systems which will ultimately alter the conditions of your life.

As Nicolas Tesla once said, if you want to find the secrets of the universe, think in terms of energy, frequency, and vibration. Your power lies in your ability to control the energy, frequency, and vibration you're predominantly in. If fundamentally you got trained into lower frequency and negative thought patterns, it will feel like an uphill climb where you're barely surviving. But once you understand how to use your empathic abilities to retrain your mind and build a new set of beliefs that support a high-quality life, accessing the energy, frequency, and vibration that heals, nourishes and prospers your life and others will become a new norm for you.

Nothing and no one has power over you; except the power you grant them.

Going beyond survival so you can thrive

Anyone can help you survive and in fact most of the information available today is about showing you how to avoid things that overwhelm or scare you. In other words it about helping you cope and survive. But a life where you're just striving to survive and keep your head above water isn't really a meaningful life. Wouldn't you agree?

You deserve to have a life you absolutely love living. A life where each morning feels like a new gift you can't wait to unwrap. And the only way to go beyond survival mode into thriving is by increasing your sense of personal responsibility. You've got to do your part and stop waiting for something or someone to come and give you the breakthrough or transformation you need.

Success and happiness come as you keep on keeping on and it's always a forward and upward movement. That means you need to align yourself with inspired action and focus always on the little steps you can take right where you stand, to feel more in control of your energy, your life, and your destiny.

The worst part about being an empath is fighting to reclaim that sense of power. It does require massive effort to win that battle but in the end, it's always worth it.

The best part is realizing that you can reclaim and restore yourself into a life far greater than your wildest imagination. It begins with a single choice to move forward and upward. It's time for you to make that choice and reach for your breakthrough. You are meant to be an example that others can emulate and as the world shifts in consciousness to more self-awareness, we sure could use more of your true Self.

So what do you say? Are you ready to start living from a place of power and complete self-acceptance?

Now, do you recall in an earlier chapter I alluded to the fact that being an empath and embracing this experience comes with some amazing advantages? Benefits that make you a powerful, valuable individual on this planet and quite frankly, it increases the "fun factor" of possessing some of your special abilities.

Here's what I mean:

The gift of being an empath, and yes it is a gift can be used practically in your daily life to benefit those you love and yourself.

Your nurturing energy helps the planet and all creatures flourish.

Regardless of what's happening globally, your ability to connect deeply with energy means you can nurture and pour nourishing, vitalizing energy into animals, people, places and the entire planet.

Your creativity can beautify the world, solve problems and add value to the global marketplace.

We are naturally very intuitive and creative as empaths and this can be utilized far beyond artistic fields. Because we think differently, innovation and creativity comes more naturally to us and as you might have guessed, the business world of today is all about innovation and creativity. So don't be shy, put your creativity on overdrive and share it with the world as you see fit. Find the thing that absorbs you and makes you come alive and allow it to turn into a creative out-put remaining detached from the outcome. It might end up being a hobby or something that makes you a fortune. Either way, give yourself permission to share your creativity with the world.

You can support and help build greater collaborations, connections and leadership structures.

Bet you never expected to hear that!

As the global marketplace shifts, a new group of leaders are emerging. People are recognizing that to be an effective leader, one must be sensitive and skilled enough to understand other people's feelings. An article posted on the Financial Post said, "If corporations want to achieve higher levels of ethics, their first step should be working on their ability to be empathic. ("Forget ethics training: focus on empathy, June 21, 2013")

Your ability to sense, understand and deeply connected with people makes you a peace maker and a valuable asset in the workplace assuming you have already grounded and worked on yourself as discussed in previous chapters. Your empathic abilities will enable you to notice the details that others miss, acknowledge other's needs and motivate people to do their best work.

The world and the marketplace cries out for more empathy and no one demonstrates empathy better than an empath.

Your strong intuition can help save lives and avoid wrong, dangerous or poor choices.

Because your intuition is so highly developed, you can always rely on that gut feeling or hunch which will never lead you astray. This can be super valuable when you or a loved one is faced with a tough or confusing choice to make. You always have that inner knowing when something feels "off" or when it's "just right" and you can use this ability to help others in every day life.

You get to be a constant authentic real human being that others can always rely on.

In a world where everyone is trying to be someone else and constantly seeks to outshine, out-perform and compete with others, most human beings are wearing masks and hardly know their truth from what they've been fed by so called gurus. Most people are imprisoned by their own egos, trying to be trendy and you by default are the exact opposite. Your high sensitivity, vulnerability and empathic abilities make you authentic, real and more willing to speak your truth. You naturally engage your heart and mind in everything your do and that has become a rare commodity in our modern society. You can be yourself and demonstrate by example to others what authenticity looks and feels like. It's always so refreshing to have a friend, who is always real, always speaks from their heart and always shows up as their real self. You can be that friend and role model.

EMPATHS, SPIRITUALITY AND PSYCHIC ABILITIES

Life is like a tree and its root is consciousness. Therefore, once we tend the root, the tree as whole will be healthy.

- Deepak Chopra

Although some people have a strong disdain for spirituality in the context of being empathic, this book would be rather incomplete and to some extent unjust if we completely disregard the connection between spirituality and the empathic experience.

Does spirituality conflict with being an empath?

The simple answer is no.

Whether you actively subscribe to a spiritually conscious life or not, you can enjoy being an empath and use your gifts in positive ways yet the underlying truth will remain unaltered for, in reality, spirituality is never in conflict with anything. Self-awareness, intuition, healing, connection are all essential for an empath and yet they very much fall into the field of spirituality.

Carl Sagan, a world-renowned scientist was quoted saying that science is not only compatible with spirituality; it is a profound source of spirituality. His statement is worth pondering over for a while as it carries great significance for us as empaths.

The need to segregate and separate things in our world has caused some of the worst conflicts to arise. This gift of being an empath is meant to be used as a force for good in this world and unless you find a way to be more integrative in your thought process when it comes to your world views, it's going to be tough feeling fully empowered in life.

Life is only one. Unity is the core of life itself, which means trying to make your powers either non-spiritual or only spiritual is still walking out of harmony with the fundamental laws of life. You are more than just a body or human being living in a human world.

You are a spiritual being having a human experience with a physical vessel to help you express more of who you really are. So whatever your empathic abilities are, embrace them from the perspective of the Truth about who you really are - whatever that means for you.

That's why earlier in this book I said my conviction is that all human beings have the capacity for empathy and depending on where they sit on that spectrum, we get to experience a little or a lot of their empathic abilities. Having determined that you sit high on that positive side of the spectrum, your special abilities come into your human experience naturally and it is your job to be grounded and intelligent enough to use them effectively.

Psychics, clairvoyants, and others with similar abilities aren't different from you, they have just fine-tuned their receptors in a specific way to access and interpret information that perhaps you haven't unlocked yet.

And you should never feel obliged to unlock anything your not comfortable with by the way, because being an empath does not automatically mean you need to be clairvoyant or psychic.

To some extent, your sensitivities and ability to connect with all the energies around you already makes you a natural psychic or clairvoyant. That's why you'll often receive a flashing thought, image or feeling of an old friend or family member that you haven't heard from in a while and all of a sudden they will call or communicate in some way. Whether you want to develop these into an actual skill that can be accurately used in the "psychic realm" is entirely up to you.

What is a psychic person?

This is a person who can supposedly receive information and communicate with spirits manifested as regular humans as well as spirits within the spirit realm. There is another type of psychic commonly referred to as a "psychic medium" who can supposedly communicate with discarnate spirits. In essence, such a person uses himself or herself as a means of communication (kind of like a telephone) to pass on messages from one spirit being to another.

What is a clairvoyant person?

This is a person who can see clearly with the mind's eye. Originally French, the term 'Clair' means 'clear' and 'voyance' means 'vision' and it enables the individual in question to clearly see events, people, scenarios and even places within their mind's eye.

Usually, the argument made is that psychics deal with thought energies while empaths deal with emotional energies but again, I want to get back to my earlier point.

The need to separate and dissect in this way only creates friction and confusion. After all, thought and emotions have an unbroken bond, why then attempt to pick a side? Rather than debate whether or not psychics, clairvoyants, and empaths are playing on the same team, focus on understanding more of your empathic abilities. Refrain from too much labeling and I would recommend you refrain judgment around the debate of whether being an empath is linked to spirituality.

Understanding your intuition, healing powers and grounding yourself:

I think it's safe to say any empath with a strong, highly developed intuition and healing powers has already ventured into spirituality and higher consciousness. For we know science cannot be able to back up with concrete proof how one is able to heal or soothe an animal in pain with just the touch of a hand. And I'm guessing they would have a hard time explaining how you're able to receive such strong intuitive messages that are almost always right on the money.

My friends and family have developed the habit of always having a conversation with me whenever they are faced with a major decision because my intuition has never failed to respond positively when summoned. If something feels off for me, I have learned to trust that information. Have you?

If yes, then you are already reaping the benefits of spiritually activating your empathic abilities. The good news is your intuitive abilities, natural healing potential and a strong sense of groundedness will skyrocket once you open your mind and consciously connect to something higher than your current level of awareness.

The fact that you can sense the energy all around you means you have the capacity to extend your awareness and sense the energy of our solar system, our galaxy, our universe. And as you connect to the power generating all these macrocosms, does it not make sense to seek the intelligence, wisdom, power, and guidance that generates it all? That is where true spiritual awakening begins. And if that's something that resonates with you, my hope is that you will get curious enough to pull on the thread of spirituality and higher consciousness. See where that leads and how that empowers your life.

Before we conclude our journey together, I want to share practical tips that will catapult you into that path of prosperity and personal fulfillment regardless of the work, relationships and goals you set for yourself.

QUICK PRACTICAL TIPS TO START THRIVING IN LIFE AS AN EMPATH

"The really important thing is not to live, but to live well...and to live well means the same thing as to live honourably or rightly."

- Socrates

Inhale... Exhale. You've made it this far. Bask in the joyful feeling of accomplishment having journeyed with me to this last chapter. We are here to equip you with life tools that you can pick and choose as you see fit to help you navigate the path of creating a thriving lifestyle.

Tip One: Start putting yourself first

As an empath, this is counterintuitive and yet I

promise you, learning to put yourself first will benefit everyone in your world. It sounds selfish and makes you question whether you're being a bad person. Yes I know those tiny voices in our heads but as I mentioned earlier, this will be part of the paradigm shifting and shedding of false belief systems. You are not a bad or selfish person when you make sure your needs are being met first before tending to the needs of others.

Do you know why in the plane the flight attendants always tell you to pull your oxygen mask first before assisting anyone else including your baby? Good. The same rule applies here. Your empathic abilities and heightened sensitivities only work when you are energized not when you're depleted.

There's an ancient proverb that says, " One cannot pour from an empty cup". How true! That's what the flight attendants mean and that's also what I mean. You need to be filled and energized at all times. Otherwise you run the risk of being "filled" with whatever junk people are dealing with.

Some of the ways I recommend you start practicing this by:

Taking up yoga classes.

Learning to meditate daily or other mindfulness practices.

Take up daily devotionals or prayer time if that's your thing.

Create your own special rituals that help you practice self-love and self-care.

Give yourself special treats often. For example, I buy myself flowers, cupcakes, chocolate or perfume often just because I know these gifts make me feel loved.

Can you think of one or two things you could do this week to make yourself feel loved?

Tip Two: Prioritize your emotions

As a highly sensitive person you can process a lot of emotions in an instant. You deeply "feel" everything. Your emotions, thoughts and sensations are pretty loud in your mind and heart. But it's not just your emotions; it's also everyone around you. That's where it can get tough because you might get so caught up helping others process their emotions that you end up numbing out yours.

Get into the habit of regularly doing a self-check. Check in with your emotions at regular intervals to make sure they are working in service of your dreams and goals.

I also want you to work on developing filters so that you can stop automatically absorbing whatever comes into your world. Be more aware of how much information you consume and raise your radar so you can quickly pick up when someone is trying to use you as a sounding board for their dysfunctional lifestyle. I'm not saying to shut people out who need your advice. What I am encouraging though is that you set a time limit so that you don't get too immersed into their world to the point of drowning.

As an empath, you tend to get caught up in other people's energies and stories. As you absorb this it becomes entangled with your own emotions, energies and story then before you know it; your body, mind and affairs start projecting lies that weren't even yours to begin with. The universal language is emotions. The most dominant emotional state you hold is the communication the universe receives and it will reflect back to you conditions and circumstances that match your broadcast. Therefore, learn to master and better process your emotions.

This can be done informally or formally but the most important thing is to remember that you are not meant to be an island. You can find ways that resonate with your personality and process your emotions in healthy ways.

If you are spiritually inclined consider arranging talks with a spiritual leader.

Do you enjoy journaling? Then buy a special book for recording your emotions and have transfer all that inner dialogue onto paper every night before sleeping.

If you like being part of a group or community then join a group counseling session near you.

You could also find a trained therapist or a life coach and do monthly sessions.

If you have a partner or friend you can trust then organize weekly coffee dates to just speak about your emotions and what you're currently feeling.

These are just a few of endless options to test out. Which option will you choose to help you build your own emotional support structure?

Tip Three: Practice gratitude religiously

Although many people talk about the high sensitivity and feeling nature of the empaths, it's usually in reference to pain and sadness. But you and I both know we feel joy and pleasure just as deeply and it's these joyful experiences that we need to capitalize on more.

In the same way all wellbeing experts advice us to create mindfulness rituals to help take care of the mind, body and soul, we also need to create rituals that help us anchor in the deep feeling of gratitude, appreciation and celebration.

There is so much power in the practice of gratitude. It has been taught for centuries across various religions and philosophies and modern science has proven the biological benefits of praise and appreciation. I know some people struggle with creating a daily practice out of this so just try a few things and stick to the one that feels most enriching to you. Remember it's about cultivating that feeling and creating that deep connection.

Buy a beautiful journal and name it " my gratitude journal" where you document 3-5 things daily you feel good about.

Download a gratitude app and use that instead just before you start the day.

Take yourself out on a special date just to celebrate being you.

Send a thank you note of thoughtful gift each week to at least one person in your life that you really appreciate.

Tip Four: Get enough sleep and downtime

Arianna Huffington founder of Thrive Global is an ambassador for sleep. She believes that everything you do, you'll do better with a good night's sleep. In her book titled *The sleep Revolution*, Arianna says, "By helping us keep the world in perspective, sleep gives us a chance to refocus on the essence of who we are. And in that place of connection, it is easier for the fears and concerns of the world to drop away."

We live in a sleep deprived community where little to no sleep proves that one is more hardworking and active in the community. Well, thanks to advocates like Arianna, the world is starting to realize the harmful effects of inadequate sleep. For empaths, this is doubly important because we absorb and process so much. Comprising the quality and quantity of sleep that our bodies need to operate at optimum levels is part of the reason we struggle so much to cope with a demanding world. I don't know about you but without my 8 hours of restful sleep, my mind feels so scattered, noisy and overwhelmed. My ability to calmly direct my energy is greatly reduced. So I've learned the hard way to stop messing with my sleep and I encourage you to do the same.

Alongside getting restful adequate sleep, give yourself time to relax and unwind after a busy day. When you attend public events, meetings or travel, make sure you set aside time to relax in quietness so you can lower your stimulation levels and restore your sanity.

How much sleep do you usually get? Is it high quality restful sleep? What are a few changes you can make to ensure you get optimum rest each night?

Tip Five: Find your purpose and vision and follow it

Simply put, find something that excites and invigorates you and pursue it with all your might. Don't wait for something to fall on your lap one day. Each moment of your life is a moment you will never get back. You get to decide whether your life is going to be created by design or by default.

In essence, as long as you're breathing you will be creating. And the sooner you start being the grand architect of your life and make up a vision that makes you happy, the sooner you can start moving in the direction where you'll feel fulfilled and satisfied.

Ever heard the old saying "without a vision, the people perish"?

That's what happens to your powers, your sense of aliveness and your dreams. They perish without a clear vision from you. If you truly want to be an empowered empath who thrives in this modern world, you must create a vision and figure out what makes you feel good. Even if you don't yet know what your purpose is or how to use your gifts, things will fall into place as you follow the path of your true bliss.

It takes boldness and determination, but I know you can do it. Here's your first baby step. Answer this question honestly, with great feeling and without reservation.

What would I love to be, do and have in this life?

Tip six: Develop a gentle way of dealing with both internal and external conflict

Our experience of conflict especially with a loved one is unbearable. We can't stand that horrid feeling and inner battle that arises whenever a disagreement occurs which is probably why most empaths keep everything in. Having to deal with anger is also not easy for us, plus we hate the thought of hurting someone else because we literally know how awful that feels.

Here's the thing though. You've done it all your life. Going along with something just for the sake of it even if it hurts you. Avoiding conflict and confrontation at all cost. Has this choice really made you a happier person?

I am definitely not suggesting you become a drama queen or king. Tantrums never resolve anything. But I do want to encourage you to find healthy ways of dealing with disagreement and conflict without absorbing the negative energy and letting it slowly consume you. Running away isn't the best solution because there's also the inner conflict that often invades to which you have no escape. So my suggestion is simple.

Find exercises, techniques and practices that help you courageously face and resolve conflicts in healthy ways.

Techniques like the verbal Aikido I shared earlier or the STOP method that world-renowned personal transformation leader Dr. Deepak Chopra teaches. S.T.O.P is an acronym for:

1. **S**top what you're doing.

2. **T**ake 3 deep breaths and smile with your whole body.

3. **O**bserve what is happening and what you're feeling in your mind and body.

4. **P**roceed with loving kindness and compassion.

In any given situation you have the power to practice STOP. Instead of running away from an uncomfortable situation or a brewing inner or outer conflict, test this technique and notice what begins to happen to your sense of empowerment.

Stepping into your own power as an empath when in the midst of a crisis, conflict or chaos is perhaps the best gift you could ever give the world and yourself. It will take practice and self-discipline but if you are ready to be a powerful force for good in the world, you'll master and overcome all obstacles that stand in the way of you growing your empathic powers including conflict and chaos.

What are some things you could start training yourself to do whenever a conflict arises?

Tip seven: Take up Yoga or Pilates

Both are forms of exercise that go beyond physical exercising. They are especially effective because they combine breathing, centering and grounding all the while strengthening your body. It's an amazing way to feel wonderful and raise your vibrational state even if you just do fifteen minutes in the comfort of your home.

Tip Eight: Set aside time daily for self-awareness

What is self-awareness? This is your ability to go within and become consciously aware of your own thoughts, feelings, physical sensations, and behaviors.

This is usually tough for empaths because we tend to be layered up by other people's needs, thought patterns and energies. Which is why you need to do this as a daily ritual. Set a specific time where it's not for physical exercise or meditation but simply a time to be with yourself, listening to yourself, observing that which is presently taking place deep within until you become more familiar with your true voice and feelings.

For example, when I shared the story of how I was smitten by this guy yet at the end of spending a weekend together I would curl up in bed completely drained and almost feeling sickly, that particular Sunday when I "caught myself" curled up in the same position experiencing the same sensations six Sundays in a row was my moment of self-awareness. I became aware of my forming habit and realized something was off. If you make this self-awareness time a regular or daily practice, it won't take you six weeks to realize you're going down the wrong rabbit hole! Now I know better and my life has changed thanks to self-awareness.

A simple way to start is by doing some mirror work, as this will give you direct insight into how you perceive yourself thereby increasing self-awareness.

Tip Nine: Fortify your intuitive guidance system.

Work on fortifying your intuitive abilities. The more your nurture and learn to trust it, the clearer the information becomes. There is no better guide on your path to help you sense when you're going down a dark rabbit hole than your intuition. It will save you time, heartache and even protect you from energy vampires and narcissist.

Your intuition will also amplify your healing powers and enable you to sense when someone you care about needs help even before they say it. It will always be the more calm, quiet voice, pay attention to it and don't allow pride or the ego distract you from receiving and taking action on the guidance given.

Tip Ten: Mindfulness practices

Daily mindfulness practices such as heart meditation, transcendental meditation, and mindful breathing will strengthen you and offer great clarity. Taking even three minutes out of your day to practice deep breathing techniques is not only good for your body, but it also keeps anxiety and stress at bay. Being mindful is one of the greatest gifts you can give yourself; use it to your advantage.

Tip Eleven: Soothe yourself using positive self-talk and conscious breath work

This is especially useful if you realize there are some unhealthy behaviors that impulsively take over whenever a stress trigger occurs. In such cases, take a few deep and very slow breaths doing your best to center yourself in your body. Allow yourself to feel your body and all the sensations even if they are unwanted. Using positive self-talk, speak words either aloud or mentally that offer you a sense of relief at that moment. Do not try to reach for words that are too far-fetched or that sound "made up". Stick to whatever resonates with you at that moment and makes you feel better.

For one person, a little motivational pep talk might be the right answer and for another, it could be a more devotional statement like "This too shall pass. Peace be still." I don't know what it will be for you but get into the habit of being your best cheerleader and this practice will become highly effective when stress hits.

Tip Twelve: Try Aromatherapy and essential oils

Our ability to process and connect with energies, smells, and other stimuli can be overwhelming, but we can also use it to our advantage. If you enjoy essential oils, test out aromatherapy as an alternative to helping you de-stress and calm your nerves.

When we inhale the aroma of oils that resonate with us, it can immediately kick our body into action causing the production of hormones like serotonin and dopamine. Just make sure you pick and choose the oils that ignite and de-stress you.

YOUR NEXT BEST STEP

It's time to plan out the new story of your life. What kind of a lifestyle would you love to own 12 months from now?

Regardless of what people say around you, the world has always been a mix of good and bad. Duality is what makes human living enjoyable. Darkness and light must co-exist in order for us to become conscious of what light is.

Therefore you will continue to hear mixed reviews and debates around whether what you possess is a gift or a curse and to be fair, you could spend the rest of your life a happy empath or a miserable burdened coping empath, barely surviving and the universe couldn't care less. So this is definitely a matter of perspective and mindset.

You will have to choose how to show up in the world and the image you want to live up to. The secret to living a life that is meaningful, fulfilling and joyful as an empath is simple: Personal evolution is what you need.

Develop a new lifestyle plan that is grounded and customized for your personal evolution:

In order for you to successfully create a blueprint for a life you love living; you'll need to engage...

- Your Imagination

-Your Attention

-Your Intention

Without these three things, no amount of planning strategizing or designing will amount to tangible results. Let's see how they will impact your blueprint.

Imagination - The best use of your imagination is to start designing the kind of future you would love to experience. What would you love to experience?

Who would you love to be? Can you vividly see this new you?

Do your best to connect emotionally and visually with this new self that is longing to be made real. The more you can connect with that new you, the easier it will be to ascertain the details necessary to make your lifestyle blueprint work.

Attention - Where attention goes, energy flows. It's that simple. If your attention is on growth, greater expansion, and personal evolution, your energy will become more concentrated along those lines and your life will continue to expand in that direction.

Intention - Be more intentional with your desire to grow and evolve. As Napoleon Hill said, the starting point of all great achievement is a burning desire. In order for you to have a thriving lifestyle, increase your success, health, wealth and love in your life you must desire to be something other than what you currently are. Making the intention that you desire to bring forth a new version of yourself and stepping into every situation each day with that intention will start to propel your life in a different direction because again, the universe is always listening and responding to the energy you broadcast.

What you need is more orderliness brought back into your daily life. You need more clarity and you need to grant yourself permission to become the architect of your life and energy.

If you're not into goal setting, that's okay. I'm not asking you to set goals here, I am asking you to become the author of your book of life. It's time to start a new chapter. One that is filled with magical meaningful moments, adventure, maybe even romance and definitely a lot of difference making in the world.

The only one who can author this book is you.

With a long list of practical tools for life, tips on how to soothe yourself and handle nasty situations you have everything you need to begin a new chapter of your life. Only the stories you tell yourself can hold you back. And the best way to prevent an old story from blocking you is to write up a new story. Focus on the journey itself, the meaningful experiences that you wish to encounter and the process not the goals.

A simple exercise that usually helps kick things off when designing a lifestyle blueprint is a process called clarity through contrast. Grab an A4 paper and create two columns. On the left, label that side *things that cause me to contract and self-sabotage*. On the right, label it *things I will focus on for greater expansion.*

An example would be jotting down on the left *"lack of sleep"* if you know that's one of the issues you want to improve in this new chapter and then, of course, the new story would be *"restful and adequate sleeping routine."*

At the end of this exercise, you will have all the old things that have kept you stuck and living a mediocre life on the left and you will have to the right all the wonderful new experiences that await you as you step into this new chapter of your life.

A few helpful things to help you craft your lifestyle in case you're feeling a bit lost on what kinds of experiences would constitute an expanding, empowered life as an empath include:

• Receiving more love.

• Giving more love, compassion, goodwill etc.

• Being of service.

• Meditating daily.

- Finding creative channels.

- Interacting more with nature.

- Using your gifts at work.

- Doing more things that bring you joy and the feeling of fun.

This list is endless but I hope you're getting the picture. By the time you're done putting a vivid, descriptive lifestyle plan of how your life will feel like and be in the next 12 months, some or all of these things on the list as well as others I haven't mentioned will all be included in that blueprint. And that will become the preview of what you can expect moving forward.

Be comfortable when things get uncomfortable

I don't want to leave you with the impression that the journey to this new lifestyle will be all unicorns and rainbows. It's bound to get uncomfortable and that's when you'll have to step things up. Part of having this documented blueprint is to have a guiding reminder and reference point to use whenever things get crappy and you wonder why you're even making all these changes.

You've got to learn to be comfortable with the

uncomfortable and you've got to find ways to keep yourself accountable so that you don't fall back into the old story. That's where things like community, coaching, and mentorship comes into play. Different options work best for different people. There is no one size fits all. Any of them could work for you as long as you figure out which one best meets your needs and you take action on that decision. The only way to being an empowered empath is getting on that path yourself and it does begin with that inner work that you commit to doing. Give yourself permission to create a new story and a new life that will benefit you and all of humanity!

MANUSCRIPT 2: THE ENNEAGRAM

The Enneagram:
The Modern Guide To The 27 Sacred Personality Types – For Healthy Relationships In Couples And Finding The Road Back To Spirituality Within You

INTRODUCTION TO ENNEAGRAM

Most of us go through life trying to deal with its struggles, challenges, and demands utterly unaware of the fact that there is a difference between the true self and the personality ego self that deals with everyday living. To "be yourself" is easier said than done in our society because we often get tangled up in mass consciousness and status quo leaving very little room for authentic self-expression and self-understanding. That's what the Enneagram is all about. It's a tool designed to help you simplify and increase your knowledge of self and in the process transcend your present level of human consciousness.

In a world layered with illusions, where everyone wears a mask on a daily basis, those who've grown tired of masquerades are thirsty for truth and authentic self-expression. This isn't something new; the quest has been ongoing for centuries now. Since the time of Socrates and even further back, there have always been those seeking the real knowledge of who they are. However, something is changing in our society.

Humanity is making a momentous leap in consciousness whereby as our lives become more complex, we experience the need to develop higher, better, more complex thinking and behaviors in order to cope. What most of us are discovering though is this approach isn't working too well.

The best way to thrive as the world continues to make a global shift isn't to seek more complicated coping mechanisms to tackle the new emerging world but rather, to simplify the way we relate to and partner up with life. In other words, we realize the better option is to seek simple solutions to our complex problems. We are learning to prioritize and appreciate this quest for truth and have become curious to discover if indeed there is more to us than what we've grown to believe about ourselves.

Have you reached a point in your life where the need to discover who you really as has increased yet you don't know where to start? Sometimes it can be tough understanding your own behavior and actions or why you react the way you do in certain situations. It's a very sobering moment when you wake up one day to the realization that you don't even know who you really are - deep inside. The pathway to the inner world is filled with great mystery and can often intimidate us especially when we've been locked out of our own truth for decades. That's where tools and proven systems become useful.

Enneagram is an ancient system and tool that was created to help those of us who care about uncovering the layers of mass consciousness so we can dive deep to discover our true self. And this book is designed to help make that journey of self-discovery and this ancient tool more straightforward, understandable, and quick to utilize.

ORIGINS

The term Enneagram is of Greek origins. Ennea is the number nine in Greek, and gram means a drawing. Translated into ordinary English, we would interpret it as a drawing with nine points.

In section one of this book, we will explore in great detail what this drawing looks like and means. For now, the critical thing to realize is that we're not just talking about some new age methodology cooked up to help you cope with the increasing stresses of life. There's more to it than meets the eye.

At first, it may just appear to be another one of those entertaining yet juvenile personality tests that don't possess any concrete basis to assure personal transformation, but if you read through the context of this material and apply right understanding to it, you'll reap the benefits of the power contained.

The earliest version of this concept is said to have been developed around the 4th century by a Christian mystic, Evagrius Ponticus who identified eight deadly thoughts plus an overarching thought he called "self-love." In addition to identifying eight deadly thoughts, Evagrius also identified "remedies" to these thoughts. (Enneagram of Personality From Wikipedia, the free encyclopedia)

Some present-day teachers of this material believe that variations of the Enneagram symbol can be traced to the sacred geometry of Pythagorean mathematicians and mystical mathematicians. Although there is much dispute over this theory and who actually originated it, the fact of the matter is that it works and is being widely used in both the business world and for spiritual growth. While the Enneagram symbol itself does have its roots in antiquity, many individuals in various ways developed the actual system that we use today not too long ago.

George Gurdijieff, a Russian mystic, and teacher is one such individual who is credited with the modern reintroduction of the Enneagram symbol.

He was a founder of a highly influential school specializing in 'inner work' and his primary way of teaching and using the symbol was through a series of sacred dances or what he called 'movements.' He believed in giving his students a direct sense of the meaning of the symbol and the process it represents but what he did not do was include the system of ennea-types, as we know it today. For us to understand who was behind this system, as we know it today, we'll have to introduce Oscar Ichazo into the story.

Oscar Ichazo is credited as the primary individual behind the contemporary Enneagram system. He was a Bolivian man who moved to Peru and later to Buenos Aries in Argentina to study 'inner work.' This led to further travel and wisdom-seeking in Asia where he gathered more knowledge across various wisdom traditions which helped him create a systematic way of understanding and applying all he had learned in his voyages. Ichazo combined teachings from Taoism, Buddhism, ancient Greek philosophy, Islam, Christianity, and mystical Judaism to form his own school of thought that utilized the use of the ancient Enneagram symbol. Thus from the 1960s when he started his teachings in Chile, the personality-based Enneagram was offered as a system to help with self-realization and transformation.

The Arica school in Chile where he taught in the 1960s and early 1970s is where he first introduced his system of 108 Enneagrams (or Ennneagons, in his terminology) but the Enneagram movement in America has been based on the first few, primarily on four of them. These are called the Enneagram of the Passions, the Enneagram of the Virtues, the Enneagram of the Fixations, and the Enneagram of the Holy Ideas. (The Traditional Enneagram, enneagraminstitute.com)

It was during this time in Chile that an American group interested in his work came to South America to study and experience firsthand his methods. One of the participants in the group was notable American psychologist Claudio Naranjo who went on to recreate his updated version of the Enneagram personality system. Although Ichazo and Naranjo started off as teacher and student, they've each gone their separate ways teaching different theories of this Enneagram system and seeing as there continue to be different schools of thought emerging on the subject, don't be surprised to find that some ideas do not always align. The fundamental objective, however, isn't to get into a debate over who is right or wrong. We are here to develop a healthy way of understanding and relating to our human psyche. This tool has proven very useful for those who practice with diligence, and it will help you better understand the people around you and yourself.

Why This Matters To You

Understanding why you behave as you do and finding a healthy way to bring out the hidden powers, talents, and aspects of you that would otherwise remain dormant can increase your personal happiness and those of your loved ones.

It's also an empathy enhancer. The more you understand why people behave as they do, the less likely you are to take things personally, get thrown off your own alignment or even misunderstand them. Now that we've become more connected than ever as a global community, there's a greater need for compassion, understanding, and empathy. At work, on social media, in public gatherings, and at home. It helps when human behavior isn't such a mystery to you because you can intelligently assess any given situation and respond rather than react when you have a bearing of the main underlying motives driving human consciousness.

Bottom line is this.

Anything we can do to know more about ourselves and become better humans is worth diving into and investing a little effort. It takes an open mind and heart, but if you're ready to soak in some new healthy perspectives, I promise to deliver the insights that can aid you.

What This Book Is About

Simply put, this book will answer the big question. Why do you do what you do whether or not it's voluntary? It unveils the underlying motives behind each of us, and it will help you gain clarity on the patterns that are not serving you so you can improve upon them as well as shine a light on the positive traits that you need to be taking advantage of.

You will finally discover the real you and become empowered enough to discern the difference between the mask you've been wearing as a form of protection all your life and the real authentic self that is you. Not only will you learn more about yourself, but you'll also begin to see the world with fresh new eyes understanding why people think, feel, behave and act as they do. This will enable you to spot those that you are most compatible with and nurture more of those relationships. In fact, I have a chapter that explicitly aids you in cultivating healthy loving relationships.

I commend you on making this choice to improve yourself and better understand your fellow human beings. Your personal success and happiness will be directly impacted by the changes and practices that you integrate as you absorb each chapter.

The book is divided into four sections. In section one, we get back to basics so you can form a solid foundation before integrating this into your life and relationships. In section two, we'll dive into the details of the Enneagram types. In section three we explore more of who you really are as well as the subtypes of the Ennea -types and lastly, I will practically walk you through integrating this into the areas of your life that matter the most. You'll also have the chance to do an Enneagram test to find out which type and subtypes most resonate with you. Now, remember, Enneagram system is a work in progress as is your life. Be easy with yourself as you go through this process and try not to get too rigid trying to fit into one specific type or subtype.

The Dark Side Of Personality Tests

A woman was performing incredibly well at her job leading a small team in a major real estate agency until she took one of the more commonly praised personality tests. After receiving the personality test results, her colleagues didn't trust her the same way. They felt she just didn't have the right personality to be in that position.

In sharing her frustration with me, she said: " after that day, anytime something goes wrong, or I make a mistake I just have this unshakeable feeling that it's because I'm this particular personality type and perhaps I should be looking for work that's better suited to that type of personality." She's worried all her colleagues also feel the same way and it creates tension that just wasn't there before in her leadership abilities. This is a real and common problem that a lot of people report once they fall into the downside of continually relying on shallow personality tests.

The mistake here is elementary. When we apply rigid labels to ourselves and others that limit the ability to do things that fall outside those test results it can be like being locked in a tiny box. I want you to avoid that erred thinking as we jump into the basics of the Enneagram system. In order for you to use this tool effectively, you must understand a very simple fact.

You are a dynamic ever-evolving human being. Your experiences, environment, and state of mind regularly change, and so does your personality type. This nine-point system isn't meant to box you into one category. All nine points are interconnected, and you may find aspects of you in several types. This is a good thing.

Being able to discover more of who you really are is possible and can be done without necessarily fitting into one rigid category. Let's get started.

SECTION I UNDERSTANDING THE BASICS AND BACKGROUND OF THE SYSTEM

THE THEORY OF ENNEAGRAM

If we truly want a better understanding of the Enneagram and how it's meant to help us lead better lives, we must at the very least take to account the primary purpose of Ichazo's work.

We have to distinguish between a man as he is in essence and as he is in ego or personality. In reality, every person is perfect, fearless and in loving unity with the entire cosmos; there is no conflict within the person between head, heart, and stomach or between the person and others.

Then something happens: the ego begins to develop, karma accumulates, there is a transition from subjectivity to objectivity; man falls from essence into personality (Interviews with Ichazo, page 9)

The actual theory of the Enneagram of personality types that he created is more than just offering you a quick test to help you fit into a specific category. It's about enlightening and prompting you to awaken to a better understanding of the structure of your soul as well as others. There is a real self and an everyday self that together form the individual you know yourself to be. Usually, we operate our entire lives from the ordinary self (also known as the ego-self) that we become estranged from that deep true self and that's where all the inner restlessness, confusion and identity crisis emerges from.

Ichazo developed his transformational teachings and methodologies to help us reconcile these two aspects of ourselves and bring back the harmony and wholeness that is our true nature.

So the enneagram is meant to equip you with a tool that helps you gain insight into your soul qualities and true essence, which Ichazo proposes to be distorted or contracted into states of ego. The theory is inspired by the western mystical and philosophical tradition of nine divine forms as discussed by Plato (platonic solids) and then further developed in the third century by the Neo-Platonic philosopher Plotinus in his work - The Enneads.

Clearly, these are far from new ideas but what we can conclude is no one had brilliantly consolidated all these different schools of thought in aiding self-awareness the way Ichazo did. The basis of his teaching is that as long as an individual is abiding in pure essence, they are in complete harmony with all of life and possess the higher essential qualities also known as the Holy Ideas.

Each Holy Idea has a corresponding Virtue. As an individual loses awareness and presence, they fall away from that pure Essence and enter the realm of personality where both the Holy Ideas and the Virtues become distorted into Ego-fixation and passion respectively.

Holy Ideas, Virtues, Ego-fixations, and Passions

According to Ichazo's theory, the loss of self-awareness leads to spiritual contraction, which gives way to ego states causing us to lose our groundedness and center. We become distorted in our thoughts, feelings, and actions disabling the connection with the Divine. He's not saying we're not supposed to have passions and ego-fixations but merely pointing out that these are lower untamed aspects of ourselves that are actually part of something bigger and better if we only learn to utilize them effectively. Once we recognize they are distorted versions of the pure Essence, it becomes our quest to restore that balance and truth in our lives. This is the primary purpose underlying the Enneagram of personality.

The objective isn't just taking a test; it's what happens to you once you take that first step of self-analysis through the test.

UNDERSTANDING THE MODERN DAY ENNEAGRAM OF PERSONALITY TOOL

Now that you have context on the purpose and origin of both the ancient Enneagram symbol as well as the concept created by Ichazo that includes the symbol that forms the Enneagram of personality, as we know it today let's shift our focus. It's time to take our attention from the basic history to the actual system so you can start seeing the value it can bring to the development of your life.

When attempting to understand and study human behavior, there are various approaches one can use. Most of them involve diagnosing pathological behaviors, and while this is important, it's certainly not a very holistic approach and does not consider human behavior in its entirety.

What the Enneagram is meant to do is offer a more holistic roadmap and a precise language to help you understand and express what you discover about yourself and others.

Although it is still unclear where the line can be drawn between Ichazo's work and Naranjo's further advancement of the system, a personal confirmation during an interview where Naranjo proclaimed that he took the work Ichazo had done to the next level by placing specific identities on the nine personality types leads me to conclude that Naranjo may be accredited to the detailed "type names" we'll be diving into in the section where we dissect each Enneagram type.

Regardless of the creator of the nine-point system, we know the twenty-first-century enneagram has evolved over the years. The detailed typing system needed to grow and factor in the psychological discoveries we've made in the modern world if it was to remain relevant.

It is our job to remember that the purpose of this tool isn't to label and categorize others or ourselves into certain fixed states. Instead, it's about opening you up to recognize the main behavioral patterns people tend to fall into, understanding that each individual can exhibit any one of these personality traits more dominantly than the other characteristics depending on their present state of being, environment and how self-aware they are.

In the interview where Claudio Naranjo explained better his role in the creation of the Enneagram of personality, as we know it today, he openly shares "When people say, "A [type] One is like this" or "a [type] Two is like that" or 'the pride type has such-and-such traits,' that comes from my own work. And that's why only people that came through my school became teachers of the Enneagram."

He goes on to say that what Ichazo had was a basic map that he helped develop to the advanced level we know it today. "I had cultivated the seed, and everything that emerged from my work was of that sort: fleshing in the skeletal information or the schemes he passed on." (Seeker After Truth: An Interview With Claudio Naranjo by Iain McNay. Watkins Magazine, 2016, October 14th)

To better understand the Enneagram of personality tool, we need to consider how the mind works. The mind wants to be strategic about handling and navigating life so you can best survive whatever comes

STRUCTURE OF THE DIAGRAM

The structure of the conventional Enneagram diagram is intended to help you visually, mentally and emotionally connect with the tool, showing you how the interrelation among the personality types works. Before we start dissecting it, I bet you're wondering why the system is numerically numbered 1-9. I was curious about it too. Does a higher numerical ranking imply that one personality type possesses more value?

Not at all! There's no difference in value between the larger and the smaller number. So just because someone is an eight does not signify they are better than a three.

ties, which can be very intriguing to an individual who has an opening mind and seeks more profound truths. As complicated as this system may appear, it is very dynamic and rather simple once you understand and connect to the diagram structure itself because it will give your mind a working mental image from which to grasp more about your natural proclivities.

When trying to discover more about yourself, others and the reason why you behave as you do, the Internet does have lots of solutions to choose from. Unfortunately, most of them don't carry enough merit to give you an answer that can actually transform your entire life. The Enneagram personality tool, however, is one of the few globally recognized systems that not only helps you learn more about your personality, it also expands your awareness to show you ways you can tap into realms that go far beyond superficial trends. Best of all, it gives you insights on how your personality type will behave when exposed to unhealthy, stressful situations as well as how good things can be once you get on the healthy path of personality development.

than just these nine types contained within the system. There are also centers and wings that play a significant role in the interpretation and understanding of your results when you do take the test.

The Centers:

The centers further arrange the nine points into three groupings. They form a triad on the diagram. Classifying the numbered points as the Instinctive center for type 1, 8 and 9; the Feeling center for type 2, 3 and 4; and finally the Thinking center for personality type 5, 6 and 7.

The Wings:

The wings are what help us recognize the fact that we are all connected regardless of type and we are also not exclusively and rigidly stuck to one numbered point. As a matter of fact, unless we embrace and develop "our wings" it's still going to be tough reaching our full potential in life.

We dive more into the centers and wings in the next chapter where you can even get a visual sense of the Enneagram to better help you connect with the system.

As you can see, there are added layers of complexi-

INTRODUCTION TO ENNEAGRAM TYPES

Based on the teachings of the Enneagram of personality system, we know there are nine points. Each with a unique type name given.

1. The Perfectionist also called the Reformer.
2. The Giver also called the Helper.
3. The Achiever also called the Performer.
4. The Romantic also called the Individualist.
5. The Observer also called the Investigator.
6. The Loyalist also called the Doubter.
7. The Enthusiast also called the Dreamer.
8. The Challenger also called the Leader.
9. The Peacemaker also called the Diplomat.

It's worth mentioning however that there are more

resonate with you. Toward the end of the book, we'll do a simple enneagram test to help you figure out where you stand and which type is most dominant in your personality. But for now, let's explore each numbered point and the enneagram structure in greater detail.

your way. The nine-pointed system of the enneagram is said to be the nine distinct and unique qualities that all human beings possess as special characteristics to help an individual navigate life (including trauma).

Your Enneagram type is the navigational tool that's with you all the time secretly influencing your behavior, perceptions, and reactions in ways you may not always predict. The more you can understand your enneagram type the greater insight you'll have about yourself and your habitual patterns of thought because you'll recognize there's one primary way that you perceive and react to things demonstrating your dominant enneagram personality. This will enable you to make an informed decision on whether or not you would like to activate other characters that you feel are better suited to the kind of individual you aspire to be.

It will also help you better discern between the real self and the ego-self in you. It's a subtle yet complex system, but it doesn't need to overwhelm or confuse you. As we hit the core of this book and uncover this nine-pointed system, take a moment to pause in between the type description to see which ones

I firmly believe that no type is better or worse than the other. Each character is unique with different attributes that can be expressed in healthy or unhealthy ways. Sure, you'll find some people desiring a specific number because according to society it's better to be that personality type, but I just don't agree with that notion. I think any symbol can become a handicap if underdeveloped. The key is to nurture the healthy aspects of whichever type you most resonate with. Don't fuss so much about what "people say" is the best personality. The best character for you is authentically being yourself and showing up as the highest version you can be.

The quickest way to understand the diagram is by starting from the outside layers and working your way in. Imagine drawing a circle. Then a triangle within the circle and let it touch all three corners. Mark the three points of the triangle 9, 3 and 6 in clockwise position with 9 sitting at the top of the circle.

All you have to do now is make six equidistant points from the circumference of the circle and designate the remaining numbers 1,2,4,5,7,8 to fill in the gaps. Be sure to do it symmetrically and in a clockwise motion. Each of these numbers represents one of the primary nine personality types. If you're doing this activity by hand, you will begin to notice that the nine points can be connected in some way by inner lines and that points 3, 6 and 9 actually form an equilateral triangle. The remaining six points can be connected as shown in the diagram below. The importance of these inner lines leads us to another vital lesson when it comes to an understanding of the Enneagram of personality tool.

At a fundamental level, the tool is used to help a person identify their most dominant type within the nine-point system. However, there's more to it than meets the eye for those who want to dive deeper. There's also interconnectedness between the nine points. So while you may find your basic personality to be a 2, it isn't uncommon to discover a little more of yourself in all nine types. This is where the Centers and Wings come into play.

All teachers and authors of Enneagram agree that we are all born with a particular dominant personality type, which emerges in childhood to help us adapt to our environment.

As infants, we don't really have a developed sense of self. The ego has not yet been activated and if you're unclear about this just spend some time in a park. Notice how the tiny infant in a pram has no sense of identity. He or she can barely tell the difference between their toes and fingers or whether a doll belongs to them or not. Then observe toddlers who are starting to become more a little self-aware. They can identify their parents and siblings but still don't have a sense of self. Then we have the five-year-olds playing together, chasing a ball around. The owner of the ball knows it belongs to her and she would probably cry if you grab it from her, but the self is still very fluid. Once they get to age seven and above, the self is well defined, and everything is about taking ownership and determining "me" and "mine." As children, we were not different. Depending on our environment, what our caregivers taught us, how they treated us and what we got exposed to, we developed a sense of self to help us fit into this world and survive.

We may, therefore, generalize that our formative years and all we were exposed to help shape our personalities. We learned to depend more heavily on the personality type that would enable us to survive and feel safe in the world around us. Some of what we ended up choosing may be wonderful, but perhaps some aspects are not healthy at all yet we still show up in the world as that person. Furthermore, it might be that we've neglected to develop and leverage the influences of the connected qualities and special abilities we may possess. That's why getting to know what center you belong to and what wings you're in possession of can be worthwhile. Let us further discuss the role of the three centers and the wings before jumping into each of the nine points on the next section.

The centers:

As mentioned earlier, Centers are segmented into a triad. These are centers of intelligence into which each of the numbered points will fall. Each center will contain three personality types. The triad consists of the thinking center, the feeling center, and the gut center.

Also known as the head, heart and gut centers respectively. These centers are designed and designated to the specific areas on the diagram intentionally. The centers are usually differentiated from each other based on how the person usually interprets life and others.

The Thinking Center:

The head types are usually too stuck in their head. They tend to withdraw from relationships. The head center is a cognitive center and the people in this triad love to think, analyze, and approach things with caution. Picture for a moment that you were at a party. If you're part of the thinking center, then your natural tendency and preference would be standing at or close to the door so you can have a better view and merely observe others.

Some authors like to refer to them as mental based

types. Their dominant emotion to keep in check is Fear.

The Feeling Center:

The heart types are usually people who engage in relationships and continuously seek out others. They are very concerned with feelings and their interactions with other people. Go back to that party scene again. This time instead of standing by the door to see who is present and what's happening around you, you'd be the first to mingle, introduce yourself to people and try to connect with as many people as possible.

Some authors will refer to these types as feeling-based types. Their dominant emotion to keep in check is Shame.

The Instinctive Center:

The gut types are instinctual. They are very direct and aren't afraid to be confrontational. People in this triad tend to act first and think and feel later. If we take that party example one last time, you'd know if this triad if your perfect fit by your approach from the moment you entered the room. Are you bold, loud, hearty and jovial in your interaction with others?

Perhaps you come off too strong which others often find offensive or intimidating. And if your the type of person that isn't shy when it comes to offering constructive criticism even if it is to the host of the party, then I'd say, this is your center of intelligence.

Some authors will refer to these types as body based types. The dominant emotion to keep in check here is Anger.

According to the Enneagram Institute, each type results from a particular relationship with a cluster of issues that characterize that center. Most simply, these issues revolve around a powerful, mostly unconscious emotional response to the loss of contact with the core of the self. (How the Enneagram system works via The Enneagram Institute)

So in other words, you have a specific unconscious emotional response that often surfaces as a result of the loss of contact between the everyday little self and the true self. The three centers having been grouped into Thinking, Instinctive and Feeling centers have as their dominant emotions Fear, Anger, and Shame respectively.

So if you take the Enneagram test and discover you're a type 6 and after a little reflection it dawns on you that fear is definitely one of the biggest paralyzers holding you back from greatness, then you've just confirmed that you're dominantly in the Thinking Center.

The more disconnected you are from your true self; the tighter the grip of fear will be because that's the dominant unconscious emotion. So when you're improving your life and working hard to manifest a life you love, it's important to keep a close watch on fear because that would be your biggest sabotager.

Each center of intelligence has certain liabilities and assets that are included in it which the assigned personality types that come under that group will possess. For example, type three falls into the "feeling center." This suggests their most dominant unconscious emotion to watch out for is shame. It also means there are certain strengths and qualities they would possess in relation to "feelings" which is why they fall into that triad.

Just so we're clear, this doesn't mean you won't experience other emotions. Think of the group you're in as containing a theme. Whatever your theme is, that will be your most dominant emotion to deal with.

The Wings:

The reason I believe wings are a significant aspect to include in your interpretation of your Enneagram results is that in truth, none of us can be entirely summed up by a single personality type.

We are unique and complex individuals. Ever evolving and changing from one moment to the next. Which means our character must also be a combination of various qualities. The wings help to integrate this concept into the system.

Although some teachers of the Enneagram argue that we only have one wing, I am convinced we must have more than one. Even if we judge it from a strictly numerical point of view, the number 1 is connected to 2 on one side and 9 on the other. The type adjacent to the 1 is what we refer to as your wing. Just as a bird or plane needs both wings to fly, you need wings to soar. These wings are supposed to compliment your core personality. They connect you to your "closest neighbors" giving you access to different resources and characteristics that can be quite useful.

Are both wings equally dominant and do you need to develop each one individually?

Yes and No. It's actually not an easy question to

answer. The Enneagram Institute provides a little insight into this. "Observation of people leads us to conclude that while the two-wing theory applies to some individuals, most people have a dominant one. In the vast majority of people, while the so-called second wing always remains operative to some degree, the dominant wing is far more important."

I think the most important thing to recall when it comes to your wings is that you will resonate more with one side and that's okay. As years go by, that might change too, and you may find yourself switching and exhibiting more qualities of the wing that's less influential. Either way, it's good to become aware of both and figure out which one aligns best with your basic personality and the human being you want to become.

An effective way of approaching and understanding your wings:

Not too long ago I walked into my favorite frozen yogurt parlor to take a break from the hour-long mall shopping I had just finished. Unfortunately, I wasn't the only one in need of this refreshing break. It would be around 5 minutes waiting in line before I finally got my turn. Rather than scowl and feel sorry for myself I decided to observe what the people in front of me were ordering with their Yoghurt Ice-cream. It was a rather exciting experience when I realized how unique we all are. Some people wanted just the plain base with no toppings at all. Others wanted four different toppings.

A teenage girl just in front of me wanted to know if she could get six different toppings! I thought that was a little too much. By the time it was my turn, I felt quite modest when I asked for a medium sized frozen yogurt with just Nutella as the topping! Yes, I'm a Nutella junkie, what can I say?

Point of the story is this.

Just as we are all uniquely different with our topping preferences, the relationships with our wings will also vary from individual to individual. The wings are not the frozen yogurt; they are the toppings, which you can choose to flavor your frozen yogurt (core personality type) with. We all have access to both our wings, and at times one will be more predominant than the other.

The more you know your preference, the easier it becomes to use your wings. Some people don't like any topping at all. In this case, we would refer to them as a light wing; some want lots of toppings or too much of one kind. Those we might refer to as strong wing/s. Others like me want to have just the right amount of toppings, and we can refer to that as balanced double wings. Regardless of your preference, connecting to your wings can help you understand the subtleties of your core personality type.

As you lean more into your wings to one side or the other, you will expand your perspective and increase your capacity to deal with tension creating a bigger potential to reframe influencers that no longer serve you. Each core personality type comes with a connected "close neighbor" on each side of the nine-point system. Some of the gifts and challenges carried by each wing will be explored in the next section as we unlock the qualities of the core personality types. Let's get to it.

SECTION II THE ENNEAGRAM PERSONALITY TYPES IN DETAIL

THE ENNEAGRAM OF PERSONALITY TYPES

Type One: The Perfectionist also called the Reformer

A person in this category is usually considered a perfectionist. He or she enjoys feeling in control and has a constant need to do what's right. Some of the core values for a type one are integrity and responsibility.

Being considered a good person is critical to those who fall into this first type, often taking a more black and white approach to everything. Something is good or bad; wrong or right - it's just that simple for them. They are more body-based and are usually more attentive to the external than the internal world.

Famous celebrities such as Hilary Clinton, Martha Stewart or even world reformers like Nelson Mandela would probably fall into this type.

Certain qualities are attributed to the typical ones. Character traits such as purposeful, principled, self-controlled full of integrity and pragmatic.

They can be quite calm and serene, but they are also known to be very critical of themselves and others. They tend to be very uncompromising and judgmental. Since they fall into the Instinctive Center, rage and anger are common experiences, but they do a good job suppressing it because they don't like to express emotions very much.

If you are a type one person, then you're more likely to be interested in doing the right thing at all times. Common sense is what you believe in, and you're very responsible often wondering what's wrong with people who don't take life seriously and own up to their responsibilities. You have high standards and tend to be an idealist doing the best you can to improve the world around you hence the common term "reformer." You're detail-oriented, precise in your manner of communication and grounded.

How to self-improve:

The best way to aid your personal growth if you resonate most with type one is to practice being less critical of yourself. Learn to release anger, rage, resentment or whatever else shows up healthily.

Learning to forgive yourself and others for mistakes will also be a liberating experience, as it will better empower you to deal with the imperfections that you become conscious of. Also, give yourself permission to have fun!

Your Wings

The Nine Wing:

Gifts:

Some of the gifts this wing brings to the strict perfectionist include but aren't limited to the following.

• That strong urge you often have to correct or improve people and things is significantly reduced.

• You are able to hold more viewpoints and be more open and collaborative.

There's an increased sense of relaxation, trust, and acceptance of others as they are.

Challenges:

Some of the challenges this wing has for the strict perfectionist include but aren't limited to the following.

• You may be less focused on tending to your personal needs and instead pour all your efforts on the needs of others, which could lead down an unhealthy path of self-neglect.

• The laid-back approach my turn unhealthy for you causing you to start procrastinating and neglecting important tasks.

The Two Wing:

Gifts:

Some of the gifts this wing brings to the strict perfectionist include but aren't limited to the following.

• You may notice your often critical attitude toward yourself and others is softened by compassion, empathy, and understanding.

• Idealism in you will be more easily expressed constructively in service to others.

Challenges:

Some of the challenges this wing brings to the strict

perfectionist include but aren't limited to the following.

• You might have an increased desire to improve people and conditions just so you can feel accepted and worthwhile.

• There's a tendency to feel victimized or taken advantage of even as you sacrifice your own needs.

Type Two: The Giver also called the Helper

This type of person is naturally very empathic, caring and helpful to others hence the term "helper."

Think of an iconic figure like Diana - Princess of Wales or Mother Teresa and you've got a good grasp of this personality type. If we dared go too far, we could even assign religious archetypes such as Jesus Christ this numbered point.

Certain qualities are attributed to the type twos. Character traits such as authenticity, compassion, generosity, possessive and caring.

Because they have such a strong need for love, they can often become people pleasers.

A type two values relationships a lot and puts a lot of energy into them to the point where he or she may neglect his or her personal needs. Empaths would undoubtedly be considered to fall into this category mostly. Being a feeling-based type, they are grouped as part of the Feeling Center, and unfortunately, this leads to the dominant sense of shame.

Often, a person in this category will try to mask the shame they are experiencing and that feeling of not being good enough by overcompensating in their interactions with others so that people can think of them as good.

If you are a type two personality, then you're more likely to be an emotional sponge always experiencing more than others, which makes you really good at supporting and giving to others. But you might have realized it's somewhat tricky giving to yourself or taking time to tend to your needs. You need to be careful not to absorb emotions on autopilot, as that will destabilize your sense of groundedness. You are a caring, communicative and naturally generous person but you must make sure it's not happening from a place of dependency.

How to self-improve:

Make self-care and self-love a priority in your life. Train yourself to start paying attention to your own needs. I know saying no and setting boundaries is difficult but you need to start recognizing when to set limits for your own mental, emotional, spiritual and physical protection.

Your Wings

The One Wing:

Gifts:

Some of the gifts this wing brings to the helpful giver type include but aren't limited to the following.

- You might feel more influenced to be more generous and giving not just to things you favor but to all things in general.

- You'll firm up your boundaries, get more honest with yourself and instead of exploding, you may find yourself redirecting those emotions to improve things in your surrounding.

Challenges:

Some of the challenges this wing brings to the helpful giver type include but aren't limited to the following.

- The influence of this wing may cause you to overwork yourself in an attempt to help the underdog and bring about more justice.

• You might experience an increase of hurt and a more significant build-up of criticism and resentment.

The Three Wing:

Gifts:

Some of the gifts this wing brings to the helpful giver type include but aren't limited to the following.

•This wing will bring you an increased sense of self-esteem; focus, effectiveness, organization and it will enable you to become a better delegator.

• You will feel confident to hold your own as well as become part of a team. It helps you realize that you don't have to do everything all on your own.

Challenges:

Some of the challenges this wing brings to the helpful giver type include but aren't limited to the following.

• As you become more involved with work and less with your inner self, you might end up neglecting your needs and becoming a workaholic.

- You might also develop the tendency to become acknowledged and be seen as "important" by those you consider influential. Hence the danger of too much pride as the motive for your work.

Type Three: The Achiever also called the Performer

An achiever, also commonly called the performer is the term given to type three personality. While there are some similarities between type one and three, a person in this category is more driven by success and having the best in life. He or she wants to be admired and validated.

Type threes are hard workers, diligent and at times even a little obsessive which is excellent because it keeps them going until they accomplish their goals. Being the best is something this personality type really cares about, and that's why they'll often become the peak performers in their chosen industry. In our modern world, individuals like Muhammad Ali, Will Smith, Tom Cruise, Elon Musk and Oprah Winfrey would undoubtedly be classified as achievers.

The qualities possessed by this person can be outstanding, and it can also be quite harmful if focused on the wrong thing. The desire to be the best at work, look good, demonstrate success and always win can make a type three super competitive, tense and might even lead to him or her to step over others just to get ahead.

Certain qualities are attributed to this type three such as driven, self-confident, image-conscious, adaptable, focused, determined, excellent, energetic and great at leadership and communication.

A type three loves learning, taking on new challenges and winning. This personality type loves to look good and is usually a smart and wonderful person to learn from especially if you want to excel in life too. They have a lot of energy and enthusiasm for life that many find contagious, and this really aids them while rising up the ranks in life or become self-made successes.

They too fall into the Thinking Center which means shame is an underlying emotional theme they continuously have to deal with. Because the three is so focused on image and outward success, he or she usually has a hard time knowing how to handle emotions, especially shame. So denial is often the preferred option for type threes.

Their coping mechanism for shame is striving to become what they believe is the most valuable and successful individual they can possibly be, in the hopes that this will dissolve that underlying restlessness and feelings of shame and inadequacy.

If you are a type three personality then productivity, high performance, and excellence move the needle for you. You love being the best and receiving recognition for it. Forward momentum, being motivated and motivating others around you to succeed comes naturally to you. There's no doubt about it, you think different, dream bigger than most and strive to accomplish more than most people. Your energy is often contagious, and people usually love being around you because you fire them up.

How to self-improve:

Take some time to self-audit regularly and gain clarity on what real success and happiness mean for you. Looking inside might be a little scary, but that's where your real power lies.

It's essential not to confuse material success with fulfillment and self-worth, and you need to draw your power from the real Source of life, not agency power. Your true value cannot come from titles, awards and external validation. And that deep sense of meaning that you long for in your life will not come from accomplishments which is why taking the time to go within and find out who you really are will enable you to emerge better and more prosperous in every conceivable way.

Your Wings

The Two Wing:

Gifts:

Some of the gifts this wing brings to the competitive achiever include but aren't limited to the following.

• This wing actually gives you the gift of finding that balance between being task or goal oriented and caring about the people. It enables you to value people and the contribution they make in your life.

• You also become more aware of your needs and see the value of prioritizing non-work relations.

Challenges:

Some of the challenges this wing brings to the competitive achiever include but aren't limited to the following.

• You may experience a lot more disappointment

and self-criticism if your achievements are not appreciated.

• You might also have an increased need for validation and gaining the approval of others especially those that are key stakeholders. Pleasing people might take a toll on your actions.

The Four Wing:

Gifts:

Some of the gifts this wing brings to the competitive achiever include but aren't limited to the following.

• One of the best gifts you will receive from this wing is the realization that self-development and taking time to understand the inner world has tremendous value.

• You will feel an increased need to be authentic, true to yourself and value relationships as a mutual exchange.

Challenges:

Some of the challenges this wing brings to the competitive achiever include but aren't limited to the following.

- You might find yourself being more moody, introverted and overly reflective.

- The amplifying feeling that "something is missing" may cause you to jump from one intense and short-lived relationship to another to help you feel good.

Type Four: The Romantic also called the Individualist

A type four person is mostly referred to as the individualist, but I also like the term romantic.

This person is super creative, sees beauty and magnificence in everything and tends to romanticize things. Think of famous individuals like Oscar Wilde, Michael Jackson, William Shakespeare or the Persian poet Hafiz, and you now have a better idea of people who would fall into this type.

Character qualities associated with this personality type include creativity, authenticity, courage, passion and emotional depth.

However, they are also considered very temperamental, self-absorbed and dramatic, always exaggerating things. There's an underlying sense of melancholy to type fours because they invariably feel like something is missing.

Fours long to be understood and treasured for who they really are but regularly feel misunderstood and unappreciated. Such a person will build an internal mental landscape where it feels more liberating and nourishing as a means of escaping the harsh, cruel world that never "gets them" or their sensitivities.

It has been said that most fours are artistic or very much into art as a means of self-expression, but whether this is the case or not, a type four personality will tend to experience a lot of displeasure and dissatisfaction in the world since they feel different and unique from those who are not like them. And they will seek to find and express wholeness and beauty in some idealistic way.

Being the most emotional of all personality types, they tend to struggle the most with the dominant emotional theme of shame. They are part of the Feeling Center and they unquestionably "feel" deeply, so their discomfort is probably more pronounced and easier to spot. However, they do try to mask this by focusing on how unique and special they are even though it may result in rollercoaster experiences of plunging into a deep depression and other negative emotions to the other extreme of beauty, joy, fantasy and inspired creativity.

If you are a personality type four, then you value individualism and personal self-expression. You love seeing someone authentically sharing their feelings, yet you notice that at times you can be really warm and welcoming while at other times you can become dry and almost cold to people. One day you can be ecstatic and soon after plunge right into depression. Envy and jealousy often creep up on you even though you don't like admitting it even to yourself.

How to self-improve:

That inner critic that's often so loud needs to be tamed and put on mute. Internalizing blame is very unhealthy for you and requires a shift in your perception and how you process negative emotions and situations.

Learn to speak your truth openly without losing control of your emotions. Find a way to balance your emotional rollercoaster so you can stop falling into the pit of despair and depression.

Your Wings

The Two Wing:

Gifts:

Some of the gifts this wing brings to the creative,

intense individualist type include but aren't limited to the following.

• The desire to be successful and look good that comes organically from this wing actually helps you to be real and resist being a drama queen or king.

• It also helps you feel more compelled to self-express in a practical way motivating you to be more active, creative and productive work that engages and inspires others. In short, you're more capable of balancing your inner and outer world.

Challenges:

Some of the challenges this wing brings to the creative, intense individualist type include but aren't limited to the following.

•There is a tendency to want to fix others and the external world instead of yourself.

• You are more prone to agitation and depression as the continued pressure to perform and become successful is added to your melancholic personality type.

The Five Wing:

Gifts:

Some of the gifts this wing brings to the creative, intense individualist type include but aren't limited to the following.

- Your highly sensitive, intuitive and emotional personality type gets balanced out with reason, logic and objective observation.

- As thinking is merged with feeling, you will become less impulsive, dramatic and more self-controlled.

Challenges:

Some of the challenges this wing brings to the creative, intense individualist type include but aren't limited to the following.

- When having tough times or feeling depressed, you'll most likely isolate yourself and hide your emotions from others.

- You might also struggle to connect with others and feel marginalized like some kind of alien around others.

Type Five: The Observer also called the Investigator

The Observer personality, also commonly referred

to as the investigator is usually brilliant, highly intellectual, keen to continuously learn and feels most comfortable in the realm of thought. This type of person tends to be very independent and enjoys solitude. He or she likes to gather information and observe patterns all around them trying to make sense of their environment and world. Individuals like Albert Einstein, Nikola Tesla, Isaac Newton, and Marie Curie are a few examples of people in this type.

Some of the qualities associated with type fives are innovative, self-reliant, isolated, secretive, curious, perceptive, scholarly, quiet and reserved. They are intense, smart thinkers and take great pleasure tending to the affairs of their mind instead of trying to fit into the world.

As the mental-based types, fives will often detach from relationships, and many consider them emotionally unexpressive. But not all of them. Some fives do care about family and relationships, but even they require a lot of time alone to recreate themselves and pursue their passions. It's not easy figuring out what's going on beneath the surface level of a five and they have an exaggerated need for privacy.

The type five personality falls into the group of the 'Thinking Center' making fear one of the dominant negative themes they have to deal with. Fear of inadequacy is one of the great battles a five must overcome when it comes to dealing with the external world as they feel unable to handle the external world actively. Perhaps this is why they tend to be detached from others and their own feelings.

Expert says that fives like to withdraw from the world due to their unconscious fear and a belief that by going into their minds and using that to penetrate the nature of our society they can better relate to it. Unfortunately, that usually doesn't work out too well for them and in their fear of being overwhelmed by people or emotions they may come across as arrogant and dismissive.

If you're a type five, then you probably value knowledge and continued education a lot especially in the topics that interest you. Some people think you're overly intellectual and sometimes you can be quite literal, but you don't really care.

Small talk and gossip annoy you to bits, and you prefer solitude. You tend to get stuck in your head, and you prefer hanging out with people who give you enough room to think things over. You like to be thorough in all that you do, and you enjoy very much engaging in deep, meaningful conversations. In fact, when you're passionate about something, you can talk about it in great technical details for a very long time. Reconnecting with the sensations and energy within your body and heart is quite a task even though you know it's good for you and above all else, personal freedom and autonomy bring you great pleasure.

How to self-improve:

Start by increasing the amount of time you spend reconnecting with your body and emotions. Your ability to access your energy and higher spiritual perceptions will only make you stronger.

Create a safe environment for yourself where you can embark on this quest regularly so that you can merge your intellectual strength with your spiritual power.

Put a little more effort on the relationships you care about.

Let your loved ones know that you care about them and be more expressive of your feelings even if it feels a little uncomfortable. Allow yourself to "feel" emotions like joy, being in love, gratitude, affection and so on. This will open up a channel for others to pour in the same into your life and help you deal with the feelings of loneliness and inadequacy that sometimes resurface.

Your Wings

The Two Wing:

Gifts:

Some of the gifts this wing brings to the quiet expert type include but aren't limited to the following.

- For a type five personality, you will have the unusual ability to connect your right and left-brain making you both intuitive and analytical.

- You will also connect more deeply in your intimate relationships.

Challenges:

Some of the challenges this wing brings to the quiet expert type include but aren't limited to the following.

- You might end up withdrawing even further from the material world and get lost in mental fantasies.

- This wing could bring with it an amplified sense of

being misunderstood and feeling like no one "gets you." This could lead to mood disorders and even depression.

The Six Wing:

Gifts:

Some of the gifts this wing brings to the quiet expert include but aren't limited to the following.

- You will have the ability to connect more deeply with groups or teams that you trust.

- This wing brings with it the courage and assertiveness of the type six, which can be very useful for you when dealing with everyday living.

Challenges:

Some of the challenges this wing brings to the quiet expert include but aren't limited to the following.

- There is a tendency to be very indecisive and fearful which could make you hesitant about getting involved in new projects or with new people.

- An increase of skepticism coming organically from this wing may have a very negative influence on your core personality causing you to be even more withdrawn and isolated from others.

Type Six: The Doubter also called the Loyal skeptic

A type six personality is always alert and keenly aware of their environment and their responsibilities. Knowing the rules and safeguarding those under their care is super important to sixes. They are very trustworthy and value being there for the people they care about. Unfortunately, they tend to feel conflicted between trusting and distrusting others. They often bounce between skepticism and certainty with a tendency to doubt themselves and question others.

They are very sober-minded people and take problem solving rather seriously to the point where it becomes a burden for them. Worry and anxiety are prevalent emotions for a six. Peace of mind is always lacking in this type, and they usually struggle with a deep sense of insecurity. If you want an idea of celebrities that could be classified as type six individuals, then think of Ellen DeGeneres, Tom Hanks, and Richard Nixon.

Some of the character qualities associated with a type six include trustworthy, responsible, committed, loyal and dependable.

The six also falls into the 'Thinking center' making fear (which often shows up as worry and anxiety) the more dominant emotional theme to watch for.

When a type six personally doesn't put their fear in check, they tend to become really suspicious of everything.

Stress levels are always high for a six and worry seems to be a constant companion as their outlook on life is often quite negative. They will dwell more on the negatives than the positives of any given situation.

If you are a type six, then you tend to pay close attention to people and problems. You're really good at anticipating problems and creating solutions, and you tend not to like ambiguity in others. But you may have realized that you can become very pessimistic, doubtful and even project some of your fears on other people. Sometimes you like to play the devil's advocate. As you grow, it's becoming more important to overcome the mind-body disconnect and even though you're cautious (maybe even phobic), you also demonstrate a lot of courage as you try to move forward even when fear has a hold on you.

How to self-improve:

Find ways to deal with the crippling effects of fear in your life and get better at facing it directly. Ask for some help and support either from an expert or trusted friend.

Learn to take things with a light heart.

Reconnect more with your body and feelings and create a safe space from which to do this so that your mental processes can be relaxed and aid in this new experiment. The more comfortable and safe you feel mentally, the faster and more enjoyable the mind-body connection will become.

Your Wings

The Five Wing:

Gifts:

Some of the gifts this wing brings to the loyal skeptic type include but aren't limited to the following.

• This wing helps you make more reasonable and sound decisions. It also makes you open-minded and capable of taking in multiple perspectives.

• You will also experience a more profound sense of inner trust and confidence in yourself as an observer and authority on your focused interested. This helps eradicate that need to seek validation from others.

Challenges:

Some of the challenges this wing brings to the loyal skeptic type include but aren't limited to the following.

- This wing may amplify your fears and anxiety or any sense of inadequacy you may have.

- You might notice a tendency to be too stuck in your head and not enough alignment with your feelings.

The Seven Wing:

Gifts:

Some of the gifts this wing brings to the loyal skeptic type include but aren't limited to the following.

- The gift of receiving this wing is that you become more optimistic. You start to see more good and become less inclined to imagine the worst of people and the world in general.

- You might notice a shift within, and without in how you approach others, how playful, lighthearted and enthusiastic you feel. It's even possible to become aware of and even laugh at your own fears as you spot them.

Challenges:

Some of the challenges this wing brings to the loyal skeptic type include but aren't limited to the following.

- The common tendency to fear and avoid pain at all cost will be amplified by this wing. This could lead to you seeking all kinds of unhealthy distractions or withdrawing even more from life.

- You might start avoiding confronting issues that require your attention and seek escapism instead.

Type Seven: The Dreamer also called the Enthusiast

The dreamer is spontaneous, a real pleasure seeker and loves to live life to the max.

Having fun is the top priority of this personality type, and they are always looking to catch the next exciting adventure that's just around the corner. Also called enthusiasts or epicures, sevens are mental based types who are forward thinkers and can't stand being limited to doing only one thing. They believe in unlimited possibilities, and it shows their variety of passions and interests. Think of individuals like Steve Jobs, Robert Downey Jr., George Clooney, and Elton John. We believe they would definitely fall into this personality type.

Some of the primary qualities attributed to those in this personality type include enthusiasm, spontaneity, resourceful, adventurous, optimistic fun and exciting.

Some sevens are extroverts though not all and in general are great communicators. Unfortunately being mental based types, they are part of the 'Thinking Center' making the dominant emotional theme of fear their most significant hurdle to overcome. And it shows up for a seven in the form of avoiding pain.

As a pleasure seeker, a seven will do anything to avoid pain and sometimes seeks distractions that turn into overindulgence. But they rationalize and justify this downward tendency just to avoid suffering. Also, since they keep shifting into the next big thing so often, sevens tend to be very scattered making it hard for them to dive deep into any single idea or stay the course in relationships and at work. True devotion is tough for a seven because he or she is such a believer in a futuristic "next big excitement" which makes it tough to narrow down his or her vision and focus wholeheartedly on one thing.

They are usually known as "big talkers" and prone to addiction and overstimulation, which, depending on the body type can be in the form of substance use, gambling, shopping, adventure seeking, or other addictions.

If you're a type seven-person, then you're very resourceful and like to think fast on your feet and switch things up when needed. Multi-tasking is easy for you and you hate the feeling of constriction.

Fun has to be in everything you do because it's who you are. You're definitely a multi-passionate human being so the commonly preached idea of just finding your "one thing" makes no sense to you. You love learning new things and approach life with an optimism that others genuinely admire.

However, you don't really care about "keeping face" or impressing people. You just care about doing your own thing and having an epic time while at it. You can bounce back from negative emotions and situations super fast. Deep down, however, you've come to the realization that you can't stand the experience of pain and it scares you. Negative states of mind, depression, and suffering whether it's your own or others' is unbearable. Introspection isn't something you enjoy, and you do go through cycles of anxiety and despair that drive you to seek out remedies at any cost.

How to self-improve:

Create a safe support structure that can enable you to face your pain, loss, deprivation or any other suffering you've been avoiding. Learn to embrace and reconnect with your inner world.

Be more present in the moment and find your peace of mind and ease without the use of stimulants. I'm not saying it's going to be easy, but you can do it.

With your level of intelligence, resourcefulness, creativity, natural strength and optimism you can be able to gain true freedom and enjoy being the expanding, adventurous human being that you were meant to be while remaining grounded in your true self.

Your Wings

The Six Wing:

Gifts:

Some of the gifts this wing brings to the enthusiast include but aren't limited to the following.

• This wing brings with it the ability for you to be more grounded and present as a seven causing you to work and connect with others in a more mindful and alert way.

• You will also experience a newfound sense of commitment to your chosen course of action, enabling you to explore things with greater depth. It creates a sense of seriousness and grounds your desire for unlimited freedom.

Challenges:

Some of the challenges this wing could bring to the enthusiast include but aren't limited to the following.

• That increased sense of duty could potentially start feeling like a burden.

• Your underlying fears may seem to be amplified, self-doubt could increase, and you might end up feeling guilty when you act irresponsibly or carefree.

The Eight Wing:

Gifts:

Some of the gifts this wing brings to the enthusiast include but aren't limited to the following.

• By leaning more to access the qualities of this wing, you'll become more assertive and step back into your real power in a more grounded way.

• You will develop resilience and in so doing become less afraid of getting hurt.

Challenges:

Some of the challenges this wing brings to the enthusiast include but aren't limited to the following.

• The insatiable urge often carried as a common characteristic of this wing may not work too well for you. If your selfish desires combine with a need for immediate satisfaction, then you could run the risk of going too far in the name of pleasure and gain. Even if it means taking advantage of others to get what you want.

• You might become more self-absorbed and look down on others treating them with a sense of superiority.

Type Eight: The Challenger also called the Leader

The best statement to sum up this personality type is "I am a master of my fate. I am the captain of my soul." Indeed this personality type believes in taking full control and ownership of their lives and being perceived as the powerful, active leader and protector. Justice, fairness, and independence are of great value to a type eight. If wronged, they will fight back with a vengeance.

Eights are body-based types giving them strong physical appetites and powerful instincts. They are bold, active in decision-making, love to be independent and are very intense people. A person typed as an eight will generally desire a grand life, and he or she will be ready and willing to go out and fight for that desire. In our modern world, individuals like Donald Trump; Denzel Washington would probably fall into this personality type. It's probable that Napoleon Bonaparte, Julia Caesar, and Winston Churchill would also be typed as eights.

Some of the qualities attributed to a type eight include, self-confidence, courage, willfulness, decisiveness, power, boldness, generosity and domination.

Eights can be difficult to handle at times especially if their personalities are developed in unhealthy ways.

They are grouped in the 'Instinctive Center' making their emotional theme anger. Eights really know how to get angry. They are very quick to anger whenever they don't get their way, or things go wrong. And in the case of unchecked anger or unhealthy personality traits, that anger can quickly turn to rage and physical violence.

They produce a lot of energy, which enables them to approach challenges with the right mental and physical attitude. The one thing an eight cannot stand is a feeling of weakness. Vulnerability (based on how society defines it) is also something a type eight would steer clear of and that makes having a deep and intimate relationship with the type eight kind of hard.

Even in their intimate relationships they still need to feel in control and powerful. When it comes to protecting their family, friends and those under their care, eights are fierce. They will go to the ends of the earth and do whatever it takes to accomplish the mission.

If you are a type eight personality, then you've noticed a tendency within you to be excessive. Some call you bossy though you don't get why. You see it as just being firm, focused, clear, assertive and leading others to victory.

Idleness, weakness, shyness are all things you can't stand in yourself and others, and you prefer when people are direct and confident as they address you. When provoked you can get outraged, and you tend to have a vengeful attitude toward people. But you always maintain an open mind; a positive mindset and you've got an abundance of energy to share with the world. Being controlled by any organization, person or system is simply unacceptable to you, and you prefer to determine your own high standards and execute on reaching them.

How to self-improve:

You have a lot of energy. Probably the most energetic of all the nine types, which means you, need to direct that energy constructively. Incorporate some self-control into your life and don't let anger and aggression remain your automatic reaction just because it's a comfortable habit.

Redefine what vulnerability means to you and learn to receive love and affection. If you need some personal assistance and support, ask for help from someone you trust or hire an expert. This is not a form of weakness. Don't get trapped in that false belief. Improving yourself is a form of strength, and it empowers you to become a better leader and protector.

Your Wings

The Seven Wing:

Gifts:

Some of the gifts this wing brings to the active controller include but aren't limited to the following.

• Tapping into the gifts of this wing will calm you down, increase your happiness and help you move through life more enthusiastically. It gives you a light heart and dissolves some of that ruthlessness often ruling your life.

• Instead of being a lone wolf trying to make it all on your own, you will start to value connecting with other people, exchanging ideas, expressing your thoughts as well as acting out your fantasies in a more harmonious way.

Challenges:

Some of the challenges this wing could bring to the

active controller type include but aren't limited to the following:

- The influence this wing may have on you could make you prone to addictions and overindulgence.

- You might also become too self-absorbed, reckless and less reflective on the consequences of your actions.

The Nine Wing:

Gifts:

Some of the gifts this wing brings to the active controller type include but aren't limited to the following.

- One of the principal gifts this wing could bring into your core personality tendency of being impulsive and autonomous is a renewed sense of unity, balance and being a bit more laid back about things.

- You will become calmer, receptive to others and instead of forcing things to happen, you'll be more at ease with just letting things unfold naturally.

Challenges:

Some of the challenges this wing brings to the active

controller type include but aren't limited to the following:

- The influence of the nine wing could lead to a build-up of tension between an increased need to withdraw from people and tasks, but then feeling guilty about it and judging yourself for doing so.

- You might fall into the trap of working too much to the point of unhealthy self-sacrifice and self-neglect.

Type Nine: The Peacemaker also called the Diplomat

The type nine personality is generally known to "go with the flow" in life. They value harmony, peace, and balance above all else and do anything possible to avoid conflict and rivalry. Individuals such as the Dalai Lama, Queen Elizabeth II, Abraham Lincoln, and Grace Kelly are all great examples of people in this personality type.

Some of the essential qualities associated with this personality type include tolerance, sturdiness, reliability, groundedness, calmness, and goodwill.

Nines are body-based types that love to get along with everyone and are pretty awesome to be around because of their friendly, warm nature. Nines can tolerate a lot and usually take an optimistic approach to every situation. They like to see the best in others and have strong faith that things will always work out for the best. They believe in a friendly universe and want to keep an open mind and heart as much as possible.

They are grouped in the 'Instinctive Center' making anger their dominant emotional theme to watch out for. All that calmness can turn into something dark and unhealthy if left unchecked. And it mostly happens in the form of suppressed and denied emotions.

Due to the inherent desire to be a peacemaker in the world, a nine usually denies the threating emotions of anger that surge up every so often. They are the most out of touch with their instinctual drives and dominant emotions within this cluster. The need to avoid conflict at all cost (including internal conflict) causes them to gloss over their unpleasant hidden feelings. A nine is also prone to inaction and procrastination especially when he or she senses unpleasant emotions.

If you're a type nine personality, then you value connecting deeply with the world and those you care about. You tend to take a conservative approach to change and sometimes struggle with a lack of motivation. Being out in nature gives you the most satisfying sensation; it's where you feel most at home.

People consider you warm, nurturing, dependable and attentive. However, this tendency to self-sacrifice carries some significant disadvantages that you don't like facing up to as it brings about discomfort. You may notice that people start taking you for granted or undervalue all that you do for them and it can be very disheartening. You have a tendency to "forget yourself" since you easily merge with others making personal boundaries really hard for you to create.

How to self-improve:

Challenge yourself to take more risks in life. Create a safe space in your life where you can train yourself to integrate harmony and conflict so that you can stop avoiding them all the time.

Pay more attention to your own needs and learn to set clear boundaries. Reconnect with your emotions and embrace the discomfort of conflict or anger as it shows up within you so you can boldly deal with it.

Seek to release rather than suppress the negative emotions that do show up. Give yourself time and space to process all your feelings.

Be more structured and strategic with your top priorities. If getting more organized is an issue then ask for help or acquire one of the many modern tools to help you better prioritize activities on a day-to-day basis.

Your Wings

The Eight Wing:

Gifts:

Some of the gifts this wing brings to the adaptive peacemaker include but aren't limited to the following.

• The positive influence this wing brings to your core personality, as a peacemaker is that you'll be more in touch with your power, independence, and authority.

•You'll become more bold, confident, influential and capable of speaking up and expressing your truth.

Challenges:

Some of the challenges this wing brings to the adaptive peacemaker include but are not limited to the following:

• There is a tendency to drift off your right path when under the influence of this wing and you might find yourself pursuing pleasure rather than genuine desires and the needs of your real self.

• You might also experience a lot of explosive aggression, rebelliousness, and anger especially if there have been unresolved issues with authority in the past.

The One Wing:

Gifts:

Some of the gifts this wing brings to the adaptive peacemaker include but aren't limited to the following.

• Your laid back, easy going approach will get an upgrade once you access this wing. It will help you create some structure around your life and activities. You'll develop a more focused perspective and lead a principle-based life.

• You will feel empowered enough to be more actively engaged in changing the things that are going wrong instead of accepting dysfunction as the standard way of life. You'll be more action oriented, but it will come from a place of purpose and certainty.

Challenges:

Some of the challenges this wing brings to the adaptive peacemaker include but aren't limited to the following:

• The increased need to do what's right and make the world perfect may lead to even more procrastination and distraction. The fear of not getting it right might actually become a huge obstacle.

• You might get caught up in the trap of doing what you "should do" or what is expected of you rather than what you really want to do.

SECTION III: INSTINCTS, SUBTYPES AND VARIANTS WITHIN THE ENNEAGRAM OF PERSONALITY TOOL

DIVING DEEPER INTO WHO YOU REALLY ARE

Just like animals, we as human beings have natural instincts hard-wired biologically that help us navigate life. Our evolution has necessitated we develop strategies that will enable us to survive and extend the reign of our species. What the Enneagram of personality does is facilitate a better understanding of the instinctual strategies we've developed as human beings, and it shows us the various ways it's impacting out behavior. This is more than just getting to know your personality type; it's about pulling back the curtain of the influences that drive you to behave as you do.

The Enneagram teachers there are three basic human instincts, and out of these three, we see a detailed dissection of how these instincts interact and combine with the nine personality types to form what is generally referred to by some teachers as the 27 subtypes. These are:

- Self-preservation Instinct.
- Social Instinct.
- Sexual Instinct.

All three instincts are within us and are behind our life strategies often ruling unconsciously. While these three are always present, one tends to be more dominant, and we tend to priorities and develop that particular drive while the others tend to be less dominant. And because we don't make it a priority to improve the least dominant one, it tends to become our blind spot.

Think of these three instincts as you would a layered cake. At the top we have our most controlling one, in the middle, we have the second that supports the predominant one, and at the bottom, we have the least developed instinct.

Again, we find some conflict even here with some schools stating they should not be referred to as subtypes while others teach they are indeed subtypes of the nine-point system. Either way, the label doesn't matter to us. We only concern ourselves with how this can help us better understand who we are and why we behave as we do. The primary instinct that we identify with combined with our Enneagram personality type help shape our path in life and the choices we make.

Since that is our core focus, we'll dive into each of the twenty-seven combinations after a brief understanding of what each instinct entails.

Self-preservation Instinct:

The need to preserve our body and its life force. Keeping away from threats. This includes our basic human needs of food, shelter, clothing, warmth and family relations.

This instinct is very focused on physical well-being, safety, material security, and daily comfort. Whenever our basic needs feel threatened by the environment, we may resort to hoarding of resources and energy to conserve what we have as a result of the external threat. We may consider this the basic primal instincts that all creatures possess as well. The drive to survive and sustain ourselves.

Social Instinct:

This Social instinct is also called "the adaptive" instinct.

It is the need to get along with others and form secure social bonds. It's about creating a sense of belonging around you.

We are seeing this a lot on social media today with memberships and communities popping up where like-minded people (who feel the need to belong) gather together. It's about focusing energy on working towards shared purposes or the greater good.

This instinct is very much about being part of something that resonates with you where you feel secure, heard and valued within that group and community.

Sexual Instinct:

The Sexual instinct is also called "the attraction" instinct.

It is the universal need to procreate and pass on our genes to continue the human race generation after generation. It governs our sexuality, intimacy and the close friendships that we treasure.

This instinct is also about directing the vitality of the life force within our bodies. It focuses on the intensity and passion contained in experiences and one on one relationships which causes us to seek opportunities that promise strong alliances, synergy, and deep connections.

This instinct is often constricted to just sexual intimacy, but it's meant to be so much more than that. It's definitely about projecting yourself into the environment and experiencing intimate relationships that are pleasurable and extend your DNA, but it can also be about passing on ideas that help you create a legacy that continues far beyond your physical reach.

When we overlay these three instincts of human behavior with all that we've discussed so far, the end result is a combination of twenty-seven subtypes further helping you relate to your personality. The set of combination that falls into our most dominant personality type helps us connect to the intricacies of our everyday behavior and preferences.

"These instincts relate to fundamental instinctual intelligence that develops within each of us to ensure our survival as individuals and as a human species.

Recent advances in neuroscience research have

confirmed the strong and often invisible way these instincts show up in modern society, for example, how a perceived threat to social status can trigger a primal fight or flight reaction."

(27 Subtypes Integrative 9 Enneagram Solutions - https://www.integrative9.com/enneagram/27-subtypes/)

Self Preservation Instinct	Social Instinct	Sexual Instinct
The need to preserve our body and its life force. Keeping away from threats. This includes our basic human needs of food, shelter, clothing, warmth and family relations.	The need to get along with others and form secure social bonds. It's about creating a sense of belonging around you.	The universal need to procreate and continue the human race generation after generation. It governs our sexuality, intimacy and the close friendships that we treasure as well as our legacy.
Type 1: The Perfectionist /Reformer	**Type 1: The Perfectionist /Reformer**	**Type 1: The Perfectionist /Reformer**
• Anxiety	• Non-adaptability	• Zealousness or Jealousy
Type 2: The Giver/Helper	**Type 2: The Giver/Helper**	**Type 2: The Giver/Helper**
• Privilege	• Ambition	• Seduction or Aggression
Type 3: The Achiever/Performer	**Type 3: The Achiever/Performer**	**Type 3: The Achiever/Performer**
• Security	• Prestige	• Charisma
Type 4: The Romantic/Individualist	**Type 4: The Romantic/Individualist**	**Type 4: The Romantic/Individualist**
• Fearlessness	• Shame	• Competition
Type 5: The Observer/Investigator	**Type 5: The Observer/Investigator**	**Type 5: The Observer/Investigator**
• Castle	• Symbols	• Confidant
Type 6: The Loyalist/Doubter	**Type 6: The Loyalist/Doubter**	**Type 6: The Loyalist/Doubter**
• Warmth	• Duty	• Warrior
Type 7: The Enthusiast/Dreamer	**Type 7: The Enthusiast/Dreamer**	**Type 7: The Enthusiast/Dreamer**
• Networking	• Sacrifice	• Fascination
Type 8: The Challenger/Leader	**Type 8: The Challenger/Leader**	**Type 8: The Challenger/Leader**
• Survival	• Camaraderie	• Possessiveness
Type 9: The Peacemaker/Diplomat	**Type 9: The Peacemaker/Diplomat**	**Type 9: The Peacemaker/Diplomat**
• Strong Appetite	• Participation	• Fusion

1. Personality Type One: The Perfectionist also called the Reformer

- Self-preservation Instinct:

The fundamental character drive here will be projected as Anxiety.

This is the perfectionist who constantly worries and seeks to control everything. Their anxiety causes them to try to anticipate risks constantly, and they like to be very prepared for everything. Attention to detail is probably an understatement for them. They are usually very hard on themselves and take things rather seriously.

This subtype prefers to avoid expressing anger even if they feel it and they will often experience and demonstrate great frustration when interrupted. The type one subtype has a very loud inner critic and tends to amplify their worry and anxiety.

- Social Instinct:

The fundamental character drive here will be projected as Non-adaptability.

Fairness and making things right motivate this subtype. They are systematic thinkers, set high standards for themselves and others and like to be an example of integrity and principled conduct.

They practice a lot of self-control and can be quite friendly while in their own comfort zone. Because they are so linear and see everything in black and white; right or wrong, it can be tough adapting to a new environment or situation. They can also become very resentful and critical with those who don't fit their idea of right.

- Sexual Instinct:

The fundamental character drive here will be projected as Zealousness and/or Jealousy.

This subtype will be highly charged, passionate and maintain high standards of self-control. They have an idealistic view of how things should be and have a tendency of wanting to reform others and make them fit into "what's right."

Rage and anger will directly be expressed by those who fall into this subtype, mainly if their efforts to improve others are restricted. They also prioritize holding the attention of their partner and usually become very jealous toward their partner or when dealing with others who seem to be doing better.

2. Personality Type Two: The Giver also called the Helper

- Self-preservation Instinct:

The fundamental character drive here will be projected as Privilege.

This type two feels privileged and unique in some way because he or she invests a lot in the creation of warm nurturing relationships. They spend a lot of time caring for and supporting others. As such there's a tendency to become self-entitled and even develop a prideful attitude demanding special privileges and approval as a result of the caretaking.

They are "cute" with a highly activated child-like spirit. This type two likes being taken care of but isn't too keen on long-term commitments. Fear of rejection is a big deal for this subtype, and they can experience a lot of hurt and abandonment when their needs are not met.

- Social Instinct:

The fundamental character drive here will be projected as Ambition.

Forming the right alliances and having great allies is essential for this subtype because they like to build their self-esteem through visible accomplishments and social approval.

This type two will use his or her seductive powers more intellectually to attune to others' needs and create a role that is central and almost indispensable within the organization, community or broader system. They like to stand out from the crowd and enjoy taking on leadership roles. They relish "being switched on" and build their influence based on the connections they form as well as their competencies.

Those in this subtype do not actively demonstrate a child-like spirit (at least not as much as the other type twos) and tend to have a strategy of giving more than they get. Seeking recognition through ambition is more pronounced in this type two personality.

- Sexual Instinct:

The fundamental character drive here will be projected as Seduction and/ or aggression.

This type two will focus all their energies, skills and seductive abilities to form and nurture powerful and intimate relationships.

This type of person is passionate, resilient, strong-willed and at times may be considered wild at heart.

They are very devoted in their personal relationships, and they don't like taking no for an answer.

This type two uses seduction, which can go as far as turning into aggression if pushed into it, to gain the desired attention and recognition.

Although they like to use body language and feeling tones that may come across as seductive, it doesn't necessarily imply sexual desire.

3. The Achiever also called the Performer

- Self-preservation Instinct:

The fundamental character drive here will be projected as Security.

This type three variation is very focused on achievement and creating material success for himself or herself. This type of person avoids being seen as image-oriented and does not like advertising his or her strengths overtly. But being successful and getting recognition for their hard work is still super important to them. Financial success and creating a sense of security around them is a huge priority for this subtype.

They work very hard and like to maintain high standards and the right image of success. This subtype three has an abundance of energy and tends to accomplish a lot.

The real danger for them is the fact that in chasing after all that success, they often lose contact with their authentic self and are prone to creating false identities and valuing themselves based on their job role or social status.

- Social Instinct:

The fundamental character drive here will be projected as Prestige.

This type three variation is more interested in being validated and receiving lots of social approval. They crave power, work hard to "know the right people" and focus a lot in gaining powerful leadership positions in the government or in business.

Prestige, praise, and influence are what this subtype will be after the most, and he or she will generally train themselves to adjust to the social norms and requirements of teams or organizations if it helps them gain influence and power. They are highly competitive and love being in the spotlight.

This particular subtype will have no issues confidently promoting their ideas and accomplishments.

Unlike the first type three who would rather not advertise their achievements and success, this subtype would actually go to the extreme to make theirs known. And to cover up anything that doesn't align with that "perfect success image."

- Sexual Instinct:

The fundamental character drive here will be projected as Charisma.

Personal power and gender identification as well as all the issues that arise from that mostly drive this type three variation. Masculinity and femininity matter a lot to them. Having the life of a "movie star" which means having that perfect outer image is what rocks their world. They are also very enthusiastic and charismatic which makes them very likable.

Being attractive to others as a man or woman is super important. But they do enjoy supporting others in their success as well and often posses that enthusiastic attitude "if you succeed, then I succeed."

The biggest challenge for this subtype despite remaining very competitive, charismatic and powerful on the outside is that those who fall into the unhealthy path of their subtype will often struggle silently with feelings of confusion concerning their sexuality. It can be tough to deal with such conflicts since so much effort is placed on appearing like a powerful performer.

4. The Romantic also called the Individualist.

- Self-preservation Instinct:

The fundamental character drive here will be projected as Fearlessness.

This type four variation while still very sensitive and idealistic will express their emotions less. In a sense, we could say they are the least dramatic of the three subtypes. But that doesn't mean they do not experience those tumultuous emotions, they just want to be viewed as someone who doesn't complain.

The truth is this type of person has simply trained himself or herself to live with suffering and pain. They know how to internalize negative emotions and prefer to be tough enough to deal with whatever comes. It makes them least likely to open up and share their feelings with others in comparison to the other subtypes, but that doesn't mean they lack in empathy. In fact, they try very hard to reach out to and support those who are suffering around them.

This subtype is very creative and deeply craves to

experience an authentic life even if that means being a bit reckless at times. They will have no trouble packing up and moving to an entirely new environment if their self-preservation trigger makes them feel like an authentic experience is elsewhere.

The biggest challenge for this personality type variation is the tension often created between the desire to build material security in their lives while still remaining fully detached from it all.

- Social Instinct:

The fundamental character drive here will be projected as Shame.

This subtype is profoundly emotional and highly tuned into their own sense of suffering. A person in this subtype will actually find comfort in suffering and expressing it to others. This tends to generate attention, support and at times admiration from others.

They often feel inadequate around social situations and easily get envious of other people's social status or when they encounter those who seem like they've already found a place where they "belong." A sense of belonging really drives them, and they strive to establish an acceptable social role where they can be heard as they share their truth.

This subtype is not competitive at all, but they do have a great desire to be understood and seen for who they really are. Their biggest issue is being able to overcome the social shame they often experience, and because they constantly doubt themselves and struggle with feelings of inferiority, there's always a hidden inner conflict going on. A person in this subtype will notice he or she has a tendency to blame others, compare themselves to others and constantly struggle with deep shame and envy.

- Sexual Instinct:

The fundamental character drive will be competition.

If the previous subtype can be termed shameful, then this variation of the personality may be called 'shameless.'

This subtype is very loud and vocal about having their needs met. They express their emotions and desires with lots of vigor. It's what I call the classic drama queen or king. They are super demanding and highly competitive. Because they believe in evaluating themselves based on how they match up to other people, competition is a big motivation for this subtype, and they will do anything to beat the competition.

Unfortunately, this competitiveness comes from a place of deep-seated insecurity and feelings of inadequacy. Personal blocks and issues are always resurfacing for this subtype because their sense of worth and value is directly tied to being able to beat those they consider strong and powerful.

5. The Observer also called the Investigator.

- Self-preservation Instinct:

The fundamental character drive here will be projected in the form of The Castle.

This personality variation is driven by the need to be very protective of the place they call home. Their personal space and privacy are very much off limits, and they have no trouble setting clear boundaries for everyone. They enjoy living a comfortable and relatively solitary life with just a few close friends.

A person in this subtype would rather sit back and observe social life than actively participate in it. They are very guarded and independent opting to cut off intimacy so as not to lower their guard and lose that sense of privacy and safety.

It's essential for this subtype to have a safe haven where they can retreat and take refuge from the world. And because they also like seclusion, having enough supplies is always a concern for them, which often leads to hoarding and living a minimalist lifestyle.

Some subtypes, however, go to the other extreme and chose to make their 'castle' wherever they are and end up traveling forever or moving from place to place. They tend to be introverts, though not all and prefer not to reveal much of their inner world.

- Social Instinct:

The fundamental character drive here will be projected in the form of Symbols.

This personality type variation is brilliant and hungry for more knowledge. Their main focus is seeking meaning and answers to the more significant questions of life. They take little to no pleasure dealing with daily trivia. Their hunger for mastery and understanding sacred symbols and language leads them down paths ordinary human beings rarely traverse.

This subtype loves to connect with and engage other brilliant minds and experts who share their ideas and hunger for higher knowledge and wisdom. Unfortunately, they often get too stuck in too much critical thinking, analysis and interpretation causing a snag in their ability to participate with others actively.

A person in this subtype will tend to be very private, reclusive and quiet, unwilling to share their personal space or inner resources but at the same time when triggered to speak on a topic they are passionate about, the same person can become very animated, speak lengthily and with great enthusiasm. It's almost as though they can go from being entirely introverted to energetically extroverted at the push of a button.

- Sexual Instinct:

The fundamental character drive here will be projected in the form of The Confidant.

This type five variation is the one related to person and connectedness the most. They too love keeping things confidential but with this slight alteration. A subtype five confidant will open up and share intimate information about their inner world and frame of mind in a private one-on-one relationship. But only to a chosen few who first undergo a series of loyalty tests.

This subtype possesses the more cool and analytical character traits and although still super secretive and reserved, once they do find that "shared chemistry" with another they will open up and enjoy the trust and connection such a relationship permits.

The primary challenge this subtype struggles with is the tension created between profoundly connecting with another person and the need to preserve autonomy.

6. The Doubter also called the Loyalist.

- Self-preservation Instinct:

The fundamental character drive here will be projected as Warmth.

This type six variation is very affectionate and warm-hearted. But fear, anxiety, and insecurity are very pronounced in them. They attempt to overcome it by forming strong relationships and bonds that help them feel secure.

Often you'll find an earlier childhood event may have created a lot of suppressed hurt causing them to be very fearful of risk-taking or making mistakes. As a result, this subtype will prefer to repress their negative emotions especially anger because they view that as a better and more cautious way of dealing with such feelings especially if they believe it might jeopardize the warmth in a relationship they genuinely need.

A person in this subtype doesn't like feeling "left out" and struggles with openly sharing their opinions. He or she prefers to stay within well-established boundaries, and risk-taking doesn't come easy.

- Social Instinct:

The fundamental character drive here will be projected as A Sense of Duty.

This type six personality variation is very focused on and concerned about living up to one's own duty. Integrity, fairness, and responsibility matter a lot to those who belong to this subtype. They believe in standing up for "the little guy" and defending the weak.

This subtype is highly rational and devoted to their work, choosing to follow the rules and procedures set in their environment. They tend to be more black and white, connect to social ideals and enjoy working toward a greater cause.

A person in this subtype is very concerned about knowing the rules and making sure that everyone understands their role too often creating clear agreements with colleagues and friends to avoid confusion or unnecessary squabble. The great challenge is the fear of rejection often brewing underneath and the deep sense of responsibility carried by their own duty which can either become a calling or a burden to them depending on how they develop their personality.

- Sexual Instinct:

The fundamental character drive here will be projected as The Warrior.

This particular personality type variation has two styles. The first style is based on overcoming the undercurrent of fear through willpower and feats of physical strength and bravery. It could also be seen in gaining intellectual power.

The second style is seen by creating beauty in their environment. Channeling their idealism and keen perceptiveness into the creation of beauty in the hopes that it will help them feel more in control and stable.

Both styles within this subtype indicate a bold assertiveness, which often passes for intimidation. A person in this subtype will unquestionably experience a lot of self-doubt, fear, and instability and will often attempt to avoid or overcome it by running straight toward it either through a focus on strength or beauty. This need for safety and power often clouds their ability to connect to their own emotions and causes them to struggle a lot with vulnerability.

7. The Dreamer also called the Enthusiast.

- Self-preservation Instinct:

The fundamental character drive here will be projected in the form of Networking.

This personality type variation loves to have good things in life and surround themselves with rich relationships, beauty, fun conversations, and entertainment.

They love planning fun projects or events, preparing elaborate meals, dining out, and sharing good ideas and even networking. Although they are more interested in family and friends, their energetic and enthusiastic approach to life and people makes them great at nurturing a "family" relation that extends far beyond blood relatives. What motivates them is making sure everyone is doing well and having the best experience with them.

A person in this subtype is generally very good at getting what they want and justifying or defending what they want to do. The biggest challenge is the tendency to overdo things, become too self-interested or overindulge in some way either with food, talking, shopping or stimulants.

- Social Instinct:

The fundamental character drive here will be projected as Sacrifice.

This subtype tends to act against the common trait of insatiability exhibited by the other sevens. They are generous and have a strong desire to create meaning and make a difference in the world. They are happy to sacrifice their own needs to serve the needs of the group, family, organization or person that they support. They have a utopian outlook on life, which usually serves them really well.

However, there is an underlying current of dependency being experienced with this subtype because they need friends and other people or group based projects to self-express and feel like they are doing something meaningful. In all their self-sacrificing nature they secretly hope to be acknowledged and appreciated for the sacrifices they make.

A person in this subtype is very generous, visionary in their thinking, focuses more on others and is drawn to anything that aims to fulfill a greater cause. Their primary challenge is the tendency to be very judgmental of others and themselves whenever they perceive a sense of selfishness showing up.

- Sexual Instinct:

The fundamental character drive here will be projected as Fascination.

Here we find the classical dreamer and idealist. This personality type variant sees the world through rose-colored filters. He or she is attracted instantly to new ideas, new people and possible adventure falling immediately into a state of fascination. But this suggestibility works both ways.

This subtype not only gets fascinated easily but as well as fascinate others. Their charm can be very persuasive and irresistible making such people great at sales and customer service.

A person in this subtype sees the good in everything and is always enthusiastic and optimistic. He or she is ever connected to the stream of infinite possibilities.

The primary challenge is having to deal with things that he or she considers dull, dreary, boring and predictable. Conditions, people and even a world that's dull are totally unacceptable and become a source of frustration.

8. The Challenger also called the Leader.

- Self-preservation Instinct:

The fundamental character drive here will be projected as Survival.

This personality variation will be more driven and focused on survival and protecting those under their care. More interested in securing physical and material success and security. These subtype eights are aggressive and excessive in their tendencies.

A typical attitude of mind is "win or die fighting." This subtype is usually seen as a very powerful, productive and direct personality never backing out of situations just because things get tough. They are also very fiercely protective of their family and friends and are often perceived as the strong pillar holding things together.

A person in this subtype is confident, secure, powerful, direct and will usually take the role of guardian, father or mother figure. He or she is very concerned with protecting themselves, the space around them and those under their care. Survival is a major concern at all times.

- Social Instinct:

The fundamental character drive here will be projected as camaraderie.

This personality variation of an eight still possesses the same aggression and excessiveness of type eight, but they channel it differently. A sense of injustice and powerlessness is active within the individuals that fall into this subtype, which they attempt to resolve by forming groups or alliances, which they become very devoted to.

They focus more on social causes and prefer to be the leader of the group or alliance, serving the people for a higher mission. Unfairness, injustice or abuse of power really triggers their sensitivities, and they feel the need to protect those under their influence against such things. They prefer to support others rather than assert their own personal needs.

A person in this subtype will usually choose to mediate his or her anger by harnessing that energy to serve the needs of the community members they serve. He or she will also want to be the "shield" loyally protecting his or her tribe from unjust authority or any other type of danger.

- Sexual Instinct:

The fundamental character drive here will be projected as Possessiveness.

This type eight variation demands control over others and loves to possess whatever they desire. They like to be rebellious and aren't afraid to break the rules. Impulsiveness rules for this subtype, and they are usually very intense people always ready to disrupt things and bring about change. They will never shy away from challenging the status quo and have a need to drive change, gain power and influence over others.

When it comes to intimacy, the eights aggression and possessiveness is still very pronounced often wanting to dominate the partner entirely.

A person in this subtype will have the same aggressive and excessive qualities that all type eights have, but with one distinct difference. They will tend to take it a bit too far.

There's a hunger for possession, which can at times be good if it's directed toward serving a worthy cause. But it can also be dangerous if directed toward something detrimental for them and others. Sometimes this personality subtype may be willing to let go and surrender if he or she feels a strong enough yearning from a partner capable of fully meeting their needs.

9. The Peacemaker also called the Diplomat.

- Self-preservation Instinct:

The fundamental character drive here will be projected as a Strong Appetite.

This personality variation is somewhat similar to an eight subtype in that they are very self-focused and concerned about meeting physical needs.

Material security and providing daily comfort for themselves is super important. Those who fall in this subtype have a big appetite for food and possessing things.

A person in this subtype is often a collector. Very focused on fulfilling their personal needs and providing material comfort. He or she loves to have time alone and can become very irritable when someone threatens their sense of balance or disrupts the daily rhythms that support their instinctual life. Material abundance is often more important than personal or spiritual growth.

- Social Instinct:

The fundamental drive will be projected as a Powerful Need for Participation.

This personality variation of the nine is the more friendly, selfless and warm type. Those who are in this subtype are usually strong, reliable, always in harmony with others and do a great job blending in with the agenda of their friends or the different social groups they become part of.

Often showing excellent leadership skills and selfless contribution, this subtype will position themselves as the mediator or facilitator, which comes naturally to them. Being part of a broader group or the community benefactor is their instinctual motive. They don't like burdening others with their personal struggles so they'll usually maintain a happy attitude and focus on the needs of others and their roles.

A person in this subtype is more interested in just feeling like they are participating in something meaningful. He or she works hard to make those they love happy and are very willing to make whatever sacrifices necessary to meet the needs of those under their care.

They are affectionate and amicable doing everything possible to be a reliable, concrete pillar for those in their care even if it means neglecting their own pain and struggles.

- Sexual Instinct:

The fundamental character drive here will be projected as Fusion or The Need To Merge.

This personality variation can be best termed as the seeker. Union with others is their instinctual motive, and that can be sexual or spiritual either with another person, nature or life itself.

This deep longing can be chaotic at times, or it can be the doorway to a transcendental experience. They tend to feel more comfortable and secure when partnered with others and usually can't stand being on their own. As a result, there can be a tendency to go along with what others demand and exclude their personal preferences.

A person in this subtype is usually very warm and affectionate possessing a deep urge to merge. Their most significant challenge is making this practical in daily living and keeping personal boundaries as well as the right focus on oneself.

How to know your subtype:

Before moving on to the next section, here are a few tips on how to recognize your subtype. For some people, this might come easy. In a matter of minutes, you could take the Enneagram test and figure out your center as well as your subtypes. If that's you, I'm glad. You're good to go. Just apply everything you've learned as you move forward in life.

If however, you're not that fortunate and still feel lost, confused or even unable to figure out your subtype instantly, I got you covered. You're not alone. This is something that happens to a lot of people. It requires more study and exploration over time, so allow the process to evolve naturally.

To some extent, I think we all identify with all three instinctual drives. So if you find that happening just know there's nothing wrong with you. After all, they all exist in each of us. But which is most vital for you overall? That's the clarity you need.

The enneagram subtypes aren't meant to be an exact science. Instead, they are intended to evoke a specific theme and make you aware of the different seasons in your life and the various motives influencing your choices. The Enneagram personality tool is a dynamic growth-oriented system and is meant to be a personal inventory that aims to pinpoint your basic fears motivations and strengths so you can facilitate your personal growth through a specific trajectory.

If you can start by confidently identifying your primary type and the main center of intelligence (one of the triads), then you'll be able to discover which of the underlying fears guide the majority of your behavior as well as your most dominant instinct.

You might even notice that the theme keeps changing as your living conditions and circumstances change, and that's okay too. Avoid becoming too rigid about this as you determine what to identify with.

Take a look at the diagram I share below. That should give you a visual representation of your subtypes. You may choose to first start by identifying yourself with the instinctual center that draws you in the most. For example: If you genuinely feel you're driven by social instinct and the need for belonging or fighting for a higher cause within a group, then you can focus on the - social instinct- and match your enneagram type with the corresponding subtype.

Self Preservation Instinct	Social Instinct	Sexual Instinct
The need to preserve our body and its life force. Keeping away from threats. This includes our basic human needs of food, shelter, clothing, warmth and family relations.	The need to get along with others and form secure social bonds. It's about creating a sense of belonging around you.	The universal need to procreate and continue the human race generation after generation. It governs our sexuality, intimacy and the close friendships that we treasure as well as our legacy.
Type 1: The Perfectionist /Reformer	**Type 1: The Perfectionist /Reformer**	**Type 1: The Perfectionist /Reformer**
• Anxiety	• Non-adaptability	• Zealousness or Jealousy
Type 2: The Giver/Helper	**Type 2: The Giver/Helper**	**Type 2: The Giver/Helper**
• Privilege	• Ambition	• Seduction or Aggression
Type 3: The Achiever/Performer	**Type 3: The Achiever/Performer**	**Type 3: The Achiever/Performer**
• Security	• Prestige	• Charisma
Type 4: The Romantic/Individualist	**Type 4: The Romantic/Individualist**	**Type 4: The Romantic/Individualist**
• Fearlessness	• Shame	• Competition
Type 5: The Observer/Investigator	**Type 5: The Observer/Investigator**	**Type 5: The Observer/Investigator**
• Castle	• Symbols	• Confidant
Type 6: The Loyalist/Doubter	**Type 6: The Loyalist/Doubter**	**Type 6: The Loyalist/Doubter**
• Warmth	• Duty	• Warrior
Type 7: The Enthusiast/Dreamer	**Type 7: The Enthusiast/Dreamer**	**Type 7: The Enthusiast/Dreamer**
• Networking	• Sacrifice	• Fascination
Type 8: The Challenger/Leader	**Type 8: The Challenger/Leader**	**Type 8: The Challenger/Leader**
• Survival	• Camaraderie	• Possessiveness
Type 9: The Peacemaker/Diplomat	**Type 9: The Peacemaker/Diplomat**	**Type 9: The Peacemaker/Diplomat**
• Strong Appetite	• Participation	• Fusion

If that doesn't seem to be yielding clear results, try another approach. You may choose to write down all the sets of nines within the subtypes that most resonate with you. Out of the sets of nine terms, you'll probably feel more drawn to one than the other two. The one that most draws you in should be the instinctual title that best describes your habits, preoccupations, and anxieties over the long-run.

My friend Joanna struggled at first with identifying her subtype. She thought she was an Enneagram personality type four with the self-preservation instinct as her dominant subtype. Her husband didn't agree. This created some doubt in her, and it took a lot of studies and deep reflection before she finally felt comfortable with her chosen Enneagram type and subtype. Perhaps you will need to do the same at first. Keep going and let the drawings below help guide you into your truth.

SECTION IV: USING THE ENNEAGRAM TO ENRICH YOUR LIFE

INTEGRATING AN ANCIENT TOOL INTO A MODERN LIVING

Having read this far, there's no denying the model of the enneagram is both simple and profoundly complex just like people.

The layers on the Enneagram system as shown in an earlier chapter then dissected into all the details you've gone through in the last two sections lead me to conclude that it would probably take a decade of deep studying to understand each of the nine types fully. Fortunately for you, it won't have to take you a decade.

In fact, all you need to get started on your self-discovery is to take a test to learn your type in the nine-point system and figure out your subtype then you can be well on your way to great revelations about your behavior, strengths and how to grow.

The good news is the more you understand why you do what you do, the easier it will become to start understanding others even if you don't necessarily know their personality type and character variation. At the very least, you will have a fresh new lens from which to interact with and understand those you encounter in your daily life. That is the power of the Enneagram of personality.

Passed on for generations from ancient times to these modern times, this system can become a handy tool for your personal growth, conflict resolution, and even character development.

Are there areas in your life you've been struggling with?

Do you have relationships that give you heartburn because you just can't seem to make them work the way you feel they should be working? Are there people in your workplace or at home you can't see eye to eye yet you know you must find a way to just get along due to the commitments held?

Is it your body that just doesn't seem to be listening to you or responding positively to anything you try?

Maybe it's the undercurrent of anger or fear or shame that you've been battling with secretly yet never quite understood.

All these issues can be improved upon with the use of this tool.

20

ACCELERATING YOUR PERSONAL GROWTH AND SELF-EXPRESSION

Personal growth and self-expression are as essential as breathing for us as human beings. Once we secure the basic needs that help keep us feeling safe and comfortable, the longing for self-expression arises naturally. It is meant to be part of our evolution and self-realization.

Self-expression doesn't necessarily mean producing art, writing, being a performer or any of that. It can absolutely include that for certain people, but at its core, it is about communicating your truth and using body language, your work, and actions and how you interact and engage with others in your world. That also includes how you dress, the way you drive your car, decorate your home and so on.

The main challenge with personal growth and self-expression comes when there feels like there's a block or a lack of inspiration and creativity to successfully get across something that you wish to portray to another in some way.

Ever been in a situation where you really wanted to express something that was burning in your heart, but for whatever reason, you fell short of full expression which resulted in a deep sense of frustration, disappointment and this feeling that you were misunderstood?

This is a common problem when we don't yet understand ourselves and the motives, instincts, and behaviors that influence our personalities. We may have an idea of what we want to communicate, but we fall short on execution or full manifestation.

I was watching a baking show the other day, and one of the contestants who was competing to win $10,000 started crying when her cake looked nothing like what she had envisioned in her mind. Even the judges had a tough time scoring her because they could just see her anguish and the fact that she just could not make manifest whatever creative idea she had at the start of the competition.

The reason enneagram of personality tool works so well to improve people's lives is that it aids them in better understanding their strengths, hang-ups, instinctual drives and warning signs to watch out for.

But it also does something few want to talk about. This tool also brings to the foreground the underlying fears that often guide our behaviors.

Don Richard Riso and Russ Hudson reveal the nine core fears that everyone needs to become aware of in *"The Wisdom Of The Enneagram."*

Type One: The fear of being evil or corrupt.

This personality type strives to be morally upstanding and virtuous in the face of external corruption. They tend to be perfectionists, always sweating even minute details. And their underlying fear is that they are corrupt. So the drive to be meticulous and act virtuously is driven by the need to prove that fear wrong. Motivated by their own sense of integrity, people who are type one personality will continuously strive to move away from corruption towards virtue.

Type Two: The fear of being unloved or unwanted by others

This personality type strives to be loved and wanted by those around them. They give, nurture and invest a lot of their time, effort and resources in cultivating relationships to overcome the inherent fear that they are not loveable. The giving and helping that comes from people who are in the type two personality comes from a place of proving they deserve to have care and love from others because they give it too much. They will continuously strive to move away from worthlessness and toward relationships that foster mutual loving and caregiving.

Type Three: The fear of being worthless and unaccomplished

This personality type aims to achieve success and status quo believing it to be the right measure of their own worth. The underlying fear here is an inherent feeling of worthlessness. This type feels they won't be desirable apart from their achievements and therefore must accomplish as much as possible in order to be desired and accepted by others. They will strive to continuously move aware from worthlessness and towards impressive accomplishments that can earn great admiration and respect.

Type Four: The fear of lacking a unique, special

and significant identity.

With this personality type comes the need to want to prove their uniqueness and individuality to others. The underlying fear in personality type four is that he or she would be worthless and unlovable if they were "ordinary" or "average." As such, they seek to create a unique identity to prove their significance in the world.

Those who are a personality type four are continuously moving aware from normalcy and towards expressions of individuality and intensity.

Type Five: The fear of being helpless and inadequate.

This type five personality strives to be knowledgeable and competent in all he or she does. They have an underlying fear of being helpless, overwhelmed and incapable of dealing with the world around them. As a result, they attempt to learn as much as they can and master as much as they can in order to feel secure, competent and capable of handling the world. Those who are in this personality type continuously strive to move away from ignorance and ambiguity and toward knowledge and understanding.

Type Six: The fear of being without support or guidance.

This type six personality strive to find guidance and support from those around them. Their underlying fear is that they are incapable of surviving on their own. As such they are always seeking out as much support and direction from others as possible. Those who fall into this personality type continuously strive to move away from isolation and towards structure, security, and guidance of others.

Type Seven: The fear of deprivation and pain

This type seven personality strive to achieve their wildest desires and find fulfillment. Their underlying concern is that others will not meet their needs and desires. Instead, they feel they must go and pursue what they want on their own. Those in this personality type strive to move away from pain, sadness, and helplessness and towards independence, happiness, and fulfillment.

Type Eight: The fear of being harmed or controlled by others

This personality type strives to be independent, powerful, influential and self-directed. Their underlying concern is that of being betrayed, controlled or violated by others. This personality type cannot stand being controlled or at the mercy of others. They feel secure and okay only when in control of their circumstances. Those who fall into this personality type are continually moving away from external limitations toward self-sufficiency and power.

Type Nine: The fear of loss and separation from others.

This personality type strives to maintain harmony and peace both internally and externally. Their underlying fear is that they will become disconnected and separated from others. They fear they will go out of sync with the world around them. As such they will do everything possible to live in harmony with other people and the world around them because this produces that feeling of security and connectedness. Those who are in this personality type usually strive to move away from conflict and pain and toward stability, peace, and harmony.

By understanding your primary enneagram type, your basic fears, and your subtype, your natural gifts become fully appreciated, and limitations don't feel so mysterious.

It becomes easier to find satisfaction in your work and relationships. You become better equipped to deal with situations, hostile environments and your impulsive behaviors. For example, if you have a deep longing to feel needed by others, you might have issues knowing when to say "No" to something because people pleasing would be a blind spot for you. So perhaps if asked at work to do double shifts you may say, "yes" even if it hurts you. In such a situation, learning to say "No" would be the healthier more satisfying answer yet you would only have this awareness about yourself if you actually understood more about your personality type.

Some people are able to spot both their primary and subtype personalities quickly while for others it requires time, study and constant self-reflection. I don't know how long it will take you, but I encourage you to begin because the sooner you do, the quicker you'll be able to create a healthier balanced and satisfying life. Before moving on to the impact and benefit of using this tool and the insights gained to improve your relationships, I invite you to take the Enneagram test and discover your primary type as well as your wings, center, and subtype.

ENNEAGRAM TEST

Let's do a quick recap of the main personality types before you jump into our interactive online test:

Type one: Reformer

If this is your primary type, your focus is to make the world "right" based on your perceptions. You are purpose driven, set high standards for yourself and are very self-controlled.

Type Two: Helper

If this is your primary type, then you are driven by the need to give and take care of others. You're generous, empathic, humble and nurturing. There's a deep longing to feel loved and accepted and at times the giving can be done in an effort to secure that state of being loved.

Type Three: Achiever

If this is your primary type, then you're more focused on being the best. You want to be perceived as successful by others. You're usually very assertive, winning is everything and your personal image matters a lot.

Type Four: Romantic

If this is your primary type, then your more artistic in all you do and you have an impeccable eye for beauty. You're more attuned to your emotions and that of others and can sometimes be quite dramatic. You're a romantic at heart, and your inner fantasy world is a sanctuary to be treasured.

Type Five: Observer

If this is your primary type then your focus in on knowledge and gaining more wisdom. You're highly intellectual with a deep hunger for new ideas and greater understanding. You can articulate new paradigms in a visionary way and although you prefer solitude, when invited to speak on a topic you're passionate about you can be very welcoming and engaged.

Type six: Loyalist

If this is your core personality type, then you're full of courage. You are trustworthy and self-reliant. You often struggle with self-doubt and doubting others, which can create a rollercoaster of emotions for you, but when you're not in doubt, you're very committed and decisive.

Type seven: Enthusiast

If this is your primary type, then fun and spontaneity is your thing. You're fun, playful and pleasant to be around. You have a very positive outlook and savor the richness of the world. You tend to get easily distracted though, and you always seem to be moving to the next exciting adventure, but when not scattered around or distracted you have the potential for tremendous accomplishments.

Types eight: Challenger

If this is your primary type, then you are intense! You like to be direct with others. Productivity, high energy and excellence in your work matter to you. You're self-determined, generous and you have a big heart. Others generally perceive you as very powerful which can at times make you seem a little controlling and intimidating, especially when you're trying to gain control and influence over others.

Type nine: Peacemaker

Peace and harmony is your primary drive if you fall into a type nine personality. You are authentic, unpretentious, and patient, get along with everyone, love to serve others and put their needs first. At your best, you can recognize, encourage and help bring out the best in others.

Take the test now and once you've gotten your results to go back to section II to read a more in-depth description of your type then jump into section III to figure out what kind of a layered cake you have.

To access the test, simply copy and paste the following link into your browser:

https://bit.ly/2xEWljI

Remember we said the subtypes are like layers of a cake that we all have?

That implies you already possess all three basic instincts, but one will be more dominant. By discovering how your cake is layered, you'll start to be more awake in your daily life choices, and some of your impulses, reactions, and experiences will make more sense.

You're personality type combined with your wings and center as well as your basic instincts layered up now give you a detailed understanding of what makes you tick. And what a liberation that becomes as you step into improving your relationships with others.

CULTIVATING HEALTHY LOVING RELATIONSHIPS

Cultivating healthy, nourishing relationships is essential for all of us. But we know how tough it can be especially in our modern society with never-ending demands. That's why it's even more critical than ever before to choose your relationships wisely.

The people you associate with and invest your energy on both personally and professionally have a direct impact on your wellbeing and success. Therefore I encourage you to get better at surrounding yourself with the right people. But who would be the right person?

A critical point to remember here especially when introducing enneagram type combinations is that no paring is particularly blessed or doomed to work out. The mistake so many people make once they learn of these enneagram combinations is they avoid or undervalue all the other types. Focusing on a specific combination does not guarantee you will be happy, nourished and in love.

What you want to establish is a different objective. You want to make sure that both you and the person in question are both exhibiting the healthy versions of your types. As long as they two of you (irrespective of type) are healthy, you're experiencing together will be amazing.

Unfortunately, this isn't always the norm. That's where self-discovery and further education comes in to play. The better informed you are about the other person's type, level of health and tendencies the greater your insight going into the relationship. This is such a great tool to help you deepen your relationships, as it will make you more conscious of your behavior both positive and negative. Once you shine the light on your underlying fears, motives and natural tendencies as well as your gifts, you will have a choice about how you respond to the relationships in your life.

Regardless of your current relationship needs,

whether that be building healthy professional relationships with clients or cultivating a passionate, intimate relationship with your significant other the enneagram tool can help you achieve your goals. It will help you to love more in the present and experience being more grounded in your true nature. You'll finally be in a position to recognize when you're acting out of fear and when you're acting out of your own truth. It will also enable you to discern the desires of your true self and those that are superficial. Once you have this level of clarity and self-awareness, it becomes easy to love and live in harmony with others. Instead of reacting whenever things aren't going as you want in a relationship, you will feel empowered to respond rather than react making it possible to love, support, encourage and bring out the best in others. More importantly, you will also become a better communicator. And we all know how important communication is in a healthy relationship.

One of my best friends recently experienced the power of using this Enneagram tool to help in her self-discovery as well as her fiancé.

There is no doubt in her mind how much Tom loves her. He is the most generous, warm, appreciative, attentive, playful and nurturing man he has ever met. They make the perfect couple because he seems to compliment her personality really well. She says, " I feel so loved and special when I'm with him. There's no one else I'd want to be marrying. But he can be rather controlling, needy and insincere at times and it was really creating friction between us."

That was before I suggested they both study the Enneagram of personality test. She had already taken the test, so it wasn't too far-fetched an idea, but it took a bit of convincing before Tom agreed. In less than a month, she told me their relationship has completely transformed. She has found new ways of demonstrating her love and feels more compassion whenever some of his weaknesses show up.

They have increased their level of intimacy and communication. Above all else, their behaviors feel less like a mysterious enemy trying to sabotage their love for each other. I can only assume with time, their self-discoveries will enrich their future marriage even more.

Although I will choose to focus more on personal and more intimate relationships, the same concept can be applied to any relationship you want to work with.

Bringing back the magic of passionate love:

There's nothing more exhilarating than finding someone who "gets you." Having someone who understands you even without uttering a word is entirely magical, and I think that's a connection we all crave. When you've discovered your Enneagram type and use it to improve as well as enhance who you really are, it will then change how you approach relationships forever.

This isn't a horoscope reading but using it to figure out the best type of people who will complement and enhance your life as a whole. I'm not saying it's an exact science, but you'll be amazed at how much harmony your relationships will experience when you learn about the personality types of your loved ones. The tendencies that usually hold you back from experiencing healthy relationships with yourself and others will no longer be a mystery. After all, the happier you become, the easier it will be to nurture healthy relationships.

Suggested combination types from the Enneagram Institute.

Type 1: The Perfectionist or Reformer

Best type combinations: 1 2 3 4 5 6 7 8 9

Type 2: The Giver or Helper

Best type combinations: 1 2 3 4 5 6 7 8 9

Type 3: The Achiever or Performer

Best type combinations: 1 2 3 4 5 6 7 8 9

Type 4: The Romantic or Individualist

Best type combinations: 1 2 3 4 5 6 7 8 9

Type 5: The Observer or Investigator

Best type combinations: 1 2 3 4 5 6 7 8 9

Type 6: The Loyalist or Doubter

Best type combinations: 1 2 3 4 5 6 7 8 9

Type 7: The Enthusiast or Dreamer

Best type combinations: 1 2 3 4 5 6 7 8 9

Type 8: The Challenger or Leader

Best type combinations: 1 2 3 4 5 6 7 8 9

Type 9: The Peacemaker or Diplomat

Best type combinations: 1 2 3 4 5 6 7 8 9

Here are a few insights on relationships for every type that might be a great starting point if you're looking to manifest new loving relationships.

When it comes to finding love and cultivating relationships:

Type One: The Reformer

Having discovered this is your type and that you are motivated by the desire to live the right way, avoiding fault and blame here's your relationship suggestion.

Embrace joy and spontaneity in your relationship by proposing a spontaneous date. Yes, I know that doesn't come too easy, but with a little relaxation and the right perspective, it can be very beneficial for you. I know this is hard to hear, but the world won't crumble if you kick your heels back and relax once in a while. Release the need to control every outcome all the time. It's also wonderful to openly share with your loved ones your core values and motivations. Let them know how much you care about improving the world and invite them into that vision. Those who "get you" will be more than encouraging and supporting of your tendencies.

Type Two: The Giver

Having discovered you're warm, empathetic and motivated by the need to be needed and loved, here's your relationship suggestion.

Fight the urge to always jump in and fix other people's problems, even if you are great at it. Learn to be there for your significant other without getting too absorbed into their world and frequently step outside the box to get in touch with your feelings. Ask yourself, "How am I doing?"

Type Three: The Achiever

Having discovered, you're motivated by success, winning big and that you're wired for high performance and productivity, here's your relationship suggestion.

You have a lot to offer, not just material success and social status. Connect with that "more" that you've got. Someone's appreciation and value of you isn't always tied to your accomplishments. Learn how to make authentic connections and don't shy away from diving deep beneath the prestige and material success you have.

Type Four: The Romantic

Having discovered you're a natural romantic with an eye for beauty and more creative and expressive than most, here's your relationship suggestion.

Learn to take control of your emotions or they will control you and create constant problems within your relationships. You can become more aware of your emotions without them consuming you. Since you know, there's a tendency to be a drama queen or king and that you're particularly sensitive when feeling misunderstood, communicate this to your loved one and help them know this side of you so they too can respond accordingly when it does happen. Use your powers of perception to put yourself in the shoes of the one you love so you can see things from their side of the table, then you'll always know the right thing to do in any given situation.

Type Five: The Observer

Having discovered you're the private, analytical type motivated by a hunger to gain more knowledge, here's your relationship suggestion.

Even though you like to be detached and enjoy solitude you also know those deep, meaningful connections where there is excellent chemistry make you happy. Embrace this. Don't be afraid to be "pulled in" close by another where chemistry aligns. Your feelings aren't too much for someone else to handle, and you do have what it takes to be good at this. Learn to reconnect more with your heart so that you can know when it's the right time to make the shift from the head to the heart.

Type Six: The Loyalist

Having discovered you're the practical, committed but ever-anxious type, here's your relationship suggestion for you.

Not everyone has a "hidden agenda." I know that's hard to hear and you have a hard time being optimistic, but it won't hurt you to give people credit once in a while. Your ability to be a great and loyal friend, ever reliable and trustworthy is a power that must not be underestimated especially in our modern world. Learn to use this power to build a robust and dependable bond with a significant other.

Type seven: The Enthusiast

With the new discovery of your type as being fun, spontaneous and being motivated by pleasure seeking experiences that stimulate you, here's your relationship advice.

Your positive, fun-loving attitude is contagious and will always attract great people to you, but you must learn to push back that urge to keep fleeing away from things too quickly. Find the courage to face what might be driving you to restless and shallow activities. Being committed to the right person isn't such a bad thing you know? You have so much greatness and wisdom to offer so start working on being more centered in body and mind.

Type eight: The Challenger

There's no doubt about it, you are fierce and intense. You're powerful, full of energy, strong and motivated by a need for control and protecting the underdogs. Here's a relationship tip that can help you cultivate amazing connections.

Vulnerability especially with the one you love is not a bad thing and doesn't weaken you in their eyes. Be okay with expressing whatever emotions come up for you. People who love you can handle the real you. The real power you possess is being able to demonstrate strength as well as tenderness when the situation calls for it. Don't hold back or fight those rare moments as they will become your most magical with the one you love.

Type nine: The Peacemaker

Having discovered you're the laid back, harmonious type who always gets along with everyone here's a piece of relationship advice for you.

Yes, you are a peacemaker, but you don't always have to "settle" for something if it's not what you truly want. And being the wonderful mediator that you are, it can be easier to express your needs and desires to another even if they differ. You have permission to voice a contrasting opinion to your significant other even if it makes you uncomfortable and uneasy. The one who truly loves you will appreciate even more getting to know your frame of mind and perspective of things. So go ahead, speak your truth!

23

MAPPING OUT YOUR PATH OF MOST JOY AND FULFILLMENT

As we said at the beginning of our journey in self-discovery and understanding the Enneagram, this typing system is based on an ancient practice that has been developed over the years to help us apply it better.

The modern Enneagram as we know it is divided into a nine-point system and subdivided into three triads or centers. The triads represent the head, the heart and the gut alternatively referred to as the thinking center, the feeling center, and the Instinctive center, which form the essential components of the human psyche.

While there are so many personality-typing systems available today, the Enneagram of personality tool stands out from the crowd and maintains its global merit for this particular reason.

It empowers you even more by offering you two pathways within your primary or dominant personality type. Not only does it dive deeper into variations you will experience even within your dominant type, but it also adds a unique aspect to things.

Namely:

You are given the direction of integration, which explains how your type is likely to behave when on a pathway of health and growth. And you're also given the direction of disintegration, which describes how your type is likely to act under pressure and stress.

This means your self-discovery goes way more in-depth than the usual personality typing systems because it gives you the power to introspect and make new conscious choices in any area of your life including relationships. It is a vital tool for anyone interested in taking their personal growth and self-awareness to the next level.

The Enneagram of personality is a tool designed to help you observe your personality (ego) and how it works more closely. Being aware of who you really are, the basic instincts that drive your behavior and the quality of character you can build to either create a healthy progressive path in life or a disintegrative one is the beginning of your self-discovery.

At a fundamental level, depending on your core personality type, there are certain passions to become vigilant of and work toward transforming. The more you reflect on your behaviors and motives the easier it will be to turn them into healthy virtues because as you recall at the start of the book, we affirmed that each of us, in essence, is pure and good.

Here is a quick recap of the passions or behaviors that may be unconsciously ruling your life plus how to transform them into healthy virtues.

Type One personality type is must work to transform his or her Anger/Resentment/Rage into Serenity.

Type Two personality type must work to transform his or her Pride into Humility.

Type Three-personality type must work to transform his or her Vanity into Integrity.

Type Four-personality type must work to transform his or her Envy into Acceptance and Equanimity.

Type Five-personality type must work to transform his or her Greed into Generosity.

Type Six-personality type must work to transform his or her Anxiety and Fear into Courage.

Type Seven-personality type must work to transform his or her Gluttony into Sobriety.

Type Eight-personality type must work to transform his or her Lust/ Intensity into Innocence/Surrender.

Type Nine personality type must work to transform his or her slothfulness/indifference into Engagement/Action.

This is why the book is laid out to help you understand what the Enneagram is and how it works before inviting you to figure out your type. The best way to figure out your type is by taking the online test that we have provided the link to in a previous chapter. By honestly answering all the questions, your top score will indicate what personality type you are. Bear in mind, you might have multiple high scores because as we said, the Enneagram is a complex, interconnected system just as a human being is complex and therefore cannot be rigidly constricted to just one strict type.

Alternatively, you could go back to the earlier chapters and read through all the detailed descriptions of all the personality types and try to decide which one is yours. If you feel like you know yourself well enough to identify your type instantly, then you may proceed on with the studying and understanding of your chosen type and all the additional information I shared in this book.

How the Enneagram can help you grow and manifest a joy-filled life.

The Enneagram is like a roadmap empowering your capacity for self-observation, and it shows you how to get to higher levels of awareness. The more you develop a clear vision of the healthiest and best version you can be, the more joyful and prosperous your life will be. It can be as simple or as complex as you desire it to be. It is recommended to start with the basics. This book covers all the basics as well as some in-depth understanding of the intricacies of the system. However, that doesn't mean our studies end there. You can still dive deeper yet into your determined core personality type, wings and subtype by venturing into what is referred to as levels of development.

In 1977 Don Riso discovered and started developing

what is today known as the nine levels of development that are the internal structures that make up the personality type itself. In other words what Don Riso teaches is that you have an internal structure which constitutes the core personality you have. Within this internal structures are layers and depending on your level, a certain behavioral demonstration of your personality type will become pronounced. The range is very wide stretching from healthy, average and all the way to the lower unhealthy levels.

This discovery was further enhanced by Don Riso and Russ Hudson in the 1990s. They are the only Enneagram teachers to include this internal structure in their teachings of the Enneagram. The book recommended in chapter nine "Wisdom of The Enneagram" can also help you better understand what these teachers mean by levels of development plus how to rise higher in your development.

They developed these nine levels of development to offer a "skeletal" structure of each type, which can be very useful for therapists, counselors and other medical professions working with a client.

It can also be very useful to you when you are trying to understand another person. By learning more about the nine levels of development within their personality type and where they are along that continuum of levels at a given time, you can be able to understand whether the person is functioning within the healthy, average or unhealthy range and support them accordingly. There are other books available online by Don Riso but I specifically encourage you to check out the Wisdom of the Enneagram if you feel ready to dive into greater details of your core personality.

This isn't a requirement. You can be able to rapidly improve your work, relationships health and overall lifestyle with the information shared in this book alone. So if you're not looking to be an expert at this, fret not. You already have all the necessary knowledge to enhance your capacity for self-reflection and higher awareness. The rest will naturally unfold as you continue to work on understanding yourself and improving the areas of weakness that come to your conscious awareness.

Now that you have taken the first few steps forward, there's no going back. Your work, relationships and how you perceive yourself can never be the same again. If you've done the inner work, you'll have a better chance at controlling yourself in whatever environment or situation you end up in. You'll also have more confidence planning for your future goals. Having this inner and outer balance is what you need to thrive as your true self in our modern world. Now that you better understand and have the tool go forth and cultivate the quality of life you've always desired!

www.ingramcontent.com/pod-product-compliance
Lightning Source LLC
LaVergne TN
LVHW092005090526
838202LV00001B/2